Derek Pearson

Up, up and away

Oxford University Press
Music Department, Walton Street, Oxford OX2 6DP

Poems

W H Allen & Co Ltd: 'Good Company' by Leonard Clark. Angus Robertson (UK) Ltd: 'One snail, two snails' from *The Singing Tree* by Mary Gilmore. Bell & Hyman Publishers Ltd: 'Mr Tortoise' by R Pope, 'The Witch' by K Watts, 'Stirring the Christmas Pudding' and 'Going to the zoo' (Anon) from *Poems for Movement*; 'Bonfire Night' by R Brighton, 'Sweeping' by J Lambert and 'The enchanted wood' by M Faulkner from *Skipping Susan*; 'Mincemeat' by Elizabeth Gould, 'Zoo manners' by Eileen Mathias and 'The farmyard' by A A Attwood from *Book of 1000 Poems*; 'The Horny Goloch' and 'Hey how for Hallowe'en' (Anon) from *Hist Wist*; 'The Donkey's Christmas' from *Moving Along* by Barbara Ireson. A & C Black (Publishers) Ltd: 'Every Thursday morning', 'Christmas Candles', 'Farmer Jackson's farm' and 'Crossing the stream' by Clive Sansom. Burke Publishing Co Ltd: 'Mud' by John Smith from *The Early Bird and the Worm*. Jonathan Cape Ltd: 'PC Plod at the Pillar Box' by Roger McGough from *After the Merrymaking*, USA rights: A D Peters & Co Ltd. Chappell Music Ltd: 'The Grasshopper', 'The Snail', 'The Spider King', 'Thelma the Thrush' and 'Norman the Zebra' from *Captain Beaky and His Band* by Jeremy Lloyd. Peter Collenette: 'Precision'. J M Dent & Sons Ltd: 'The Pines' by Margaret Mahy from *The First Margaret Mahy Story Book*, USA rights: reprinted by permission of Helen Hoke Associates. André Deutsch Ltd: 'The Frugal Fly' from *Riddles, Rhymes and Rigmaroles* by John Cunliffe. Dobson Books Ltd: 'The city' from *The Big Book to Grow on* edited by Bertl Hayde. Dolphin Concert Productions Ltd: '*I wish I'd looked after my teeth*' by Pam Ayres. Doubleday & Company Inc: 'The Green Spring' by Shan Mei from *Twentieth Century Chinese Poetry* translated by Kai-yu Hsu, copyright © 1963 by Kai-yu Hsu, reprinted by permission of Doubleday & Company Inc. Epworth Press: 'The Apple Man' by Helen Clyde from A Pocketful of Rhymes. Gavin Ewart: 'The weather'. Faber and Faber Ltd: 'Glass Falling' by Louis MacNeice from *The Collected Poems of Louis MacNeice*. Aileen Fisher: 'After a bath' and 'Upside down' from *Up the Windy Hill* published by Abelard Press, New York 1953, © Aileen Fisher, copyright renewed 1981; 'Old Man Moon' and 'Clouds' from *In the Woods, In the Meadow, In the Sky* published by Charles Scribner's Sons, New York 1965, © Aileen Fisher; 'The Spinning Earth' from *I Wonder How, I Wonder Why* published by Abelard-Schuman, New York 1962, © Aileen Fisher. George Allen & Unwin: 'Errantry' (eight lines) and 'Oliphaunt' (one verse) from *The Adventures of Tom Bombadil* by J R R Tolkien, copyright © 1962 by George Allen & Unwin Ltd, USA rights: reprinted by permission of Houghton Mifflin Company. Granada Publishing Ltd: 'In Just' and 'Hist Whist' by e e cummings, USA and Canadian rights: Liveright Publishing Corporation reprinted from *Tulips and Chimneys* by e e cummings, edited by George James Firmage by permission of Liveright Publishing Corporation. Copyright 1923, 1925 and renewed 1951, 1953 by E E Cummings. Copyright © 1973, 1976 by The Trustees for the E E Cummings Trust. Copyright © 1973, 1976 by George James Firmage. Harcourt Brace Jovanovich Inc: 'Fog' from *Chicago Poems* by Carl Sandburg, copyright 1916 by Holt Rinehart and Winston Inc, copyright 1944 by Carl Sandburg, reprinted by permission of Harcourt Brace Jovanovich Inc; 'Stars, Songs, Faces' from *Smoke and Steel* by Carl Sandburg, copyright 1920 by Harcourt Brace Jovanovich Inc, renewed 1948 by Carl Sandburg, reprinted by permission of the publisher; 'Circles' from *The People, Yes* by Carl Sandburg, copyright 1936 by Harcourt Brace Jovanovich Inc, renewed 1964 by Carl Sandburg, reprinted by permission of the publisher. Harper & Row Publishers Inc: 'Engineers' from *Puddin' an' Pie* by Jimmy Garthwaite, copyright 1929 by Harper & Row publishers Inc, renewed 1957 by Merle Garthwaite, reprinted by permission of the publisher. Harrap Ltd: 'Let's take a ride' from *Singing Fun* by Lucille Wood and Louise Scott, USA and Canadian rights: Bowmar/Noble Publishers Inc, copyright 1954. Mrs Ann Hay: 'The growing river', 'Postman's knock' and 'Chop chop' by Rodney Bennett. William Heinemann Ltd: 'Beach Leaves' from *The Wandering Moon* by James Reeves, 'Twenty-six letters' from *Complete Poems for Children* by James Reeves, and 'Slowly' from *Hurdy Gurdy* by James Reeves. David Higham Associates Ltd: 'The Innkeeper's wife' from *The Witnesses* by Clive Sansom published by Methuen; 'The tide in the river' from *Silver Sand and Snow* by Eleanor Farjeon published by Michael Joseph. M & J Hobbs Publishers: 'The bumble bee' by Joyce Grenfell from *Milligan's Ark*. Roderick Hunt: 'Flute Girl'. Barbara Ireson: 'At the supermarket' and 'The grocers' © Barbara Ireson. John Kitching: 'Lonely boy' from *A First Poetry Book*, Oxford University Press. Hazel Lindon: 'Sink song' by J A Lindon © Hazel Lindon. James MacGibbon: 'Fafnir and the Knights' (seven verses) by Stevie Smith from *The Collected Poems of Stevie Smith* published by Allen Lane, USA rights: New Directions Publishing Corporation from *Selected Poems of Stevie Smith*, copyright © 1964 by Stevie Smith, reprinted by permission of New Directions Publishing Corporation. Macmillan, London and Basingstoke: 'The horse' and 'The chameleon' by Alan Brownjohn from *Brownjohn's Beasts*; 'Paper boats' by Rabindranath Tagore from *Collected Poems and Plays*, USA rights: reprinted with the permission of Macmillan Publishing Company in from *Collected Poems and Plays* by Rabindranath Tagore, copyright 1913 by Macmillan Publishing Co Inc, renewed 1941 by Rabindranath Tagore; 'The Prayer of the Donkey' from *Prayers from the Ark* by Carmen Bernos de Gasztold, USA rights: Viking Penguin Inc from *Prayers from the Ark* by Carmen Bernos de Gasztold, translated by Rumer Godden, English text copyright © 1962 by Rumer Godden, reprinted by permission of Viking Penguin Inc. Spike Milligan: 'Bump' © Spike Milligan. Oxford University Press: 'The Magic Seeds' from *The Blackbird in the Lilac* by James Reeves (1952), 'The Apple Tree' from *A Realistic Approach to Number Teaching* by Dorothy Williams (1948). Paxton Music Ltd: 'To and fro' by Jennifer Day from *Little Songs with Rhythmic Movement* reproduced by permission of Paxton Music Ltd. Penguin Books Ltd: 'It's dark outside. . .' by Nancy Chambers from *Stickleback, Stickleback* by Nancy Chambers (Kestrel Books 1977), copyright © Nancy Chambers 1977; 'Busy day' and 'Fork week' by Michael Rosen from *You Tell Me* by Roger McGough and Michael Rosen (Puffin Books 1981) pp. 36–37, 52–53, Michael Rosen poems copyright © Michael Rosen 1979, This collection copyright © Penguin Books Ltd 1979. A D Peters Ltd: 'Cousin Nell' by Roger McGough. Richard Rieu: 'The green train' and 'The paint box' by E V Rieu. Vernon Scannell: 'Death of a snowman' © Vernon Scannell. Jacqueline Segal: 'A blink'. Ian Serraillier: 'The tickle rhyme' © 1946. The Society of Authors and the Literary Trustees of Walter de la Mare: 'The storm' by Walter de la Mare, reprinted with the permission of the Literary Trustees of Walter de la Mare and the Society of Authors as their representative. Stainer & Bell Ltd: 'Help me wind my ball of wool' by Ann Elliot from *Fingers and Thumbs* (Galaxy), USA rights: Galaxy Music Corporation. Shirley K Vickery: 'Flicker flacker flack' © Shirley Vickery. Ward Lock Educational Ltd: 'Isn't dressing depressing' and 'Yesterday' from *Knock at the Door* © Ward Lock Educational 1980. Raymond Wilson: 'Two's company' © Raymond Wilson. Harriet Wasserman Literary Agency: 'Hello's a handy word', 'Eggs are laid by turkeys' and 'Good morning when it's morning' from *Nuts to You and Nuts to Me* by Mary Ann Hoberman, USA and Canadian rights: Alfred A Knopf Inc.

Songs

Abingdon Press: 'Days of the week' from *Music Activities for Retarded Children* by David R Ginglend and Winifred E Stiles, copyright © 1965 by Abingdon Press, used by Permission. Amadeo-Brio Music Inc: 'Morning Town Ride' by Malvina Reynolds published by Amadeo-Brio Music Inc (Leosong). Bowman/Noble Publishers: 'Pick up a leaf' words by Lucille Wood, reprinted by permission of the author and publisher from *Rhythms to Reading* copyright © 1969 by Bowmar/Noble Publishers, a Division of The Economy Company, Oklahoma City, USA. Carlin Music Corporation: 'Up, up and away' by Jim Webb, used by kind permission of Carlin Music Corp, 14 New Burlington Street, London W1X 2LR for the territory of the United Kingdom, British Commonwealth (excluding Canada/Australasia) and the Republic of Ireland, USA rights: © 1967 The EMP Company, used by permission, all rights reserved. Chappell Music Ltd: 'Sing a Rainbow' by Arthur Hamilton. Dash Music Co Ltd: 'Nellie the elephant' words by Ralph Butler, music by Peter Hart, © 1956 Dash Music Co Ltd, 37 Soho Square, London W1V 5DG, all rights reserved, used by permission. EMI Music Publishing Ltd: 'Happy Birthday' © 1939 Summy Birchard Co (USA) sub published by Keith Prowse Music Publishing Ltd, reproduced by permission of EMI Music Publishing Ltd. Essex Music Group: 'Going to the zoo' by Tom Paxton, used by permission of Harmony Music Ltd; 'Black and White' words by David Arkin, music by Earl Robinson, used by permission of Durham Music Ltd. McClelland and Stewart Ltd: 'Popeye the sailor man' by Sammy Lerner from *Sally go round the sun* by Edith Fowke, used by permission of the Canadian Publishers, McClelland and Stewart, Toronto. Oxford University Press: 'Nature Carol'. Brenda Piper: 'The way we learn' and 'Travelling song'. Gwen Rosman: 'Apple song' and 'Right hand, left hand'. Warner Bros Music Ltd: 'Puff the magic dragon' by Peter Yarrow.

Every effort has been made to trace and acknowledge copyright owners. If any right has been omitted, the publishers offer their apologies and will rectify this in subsequent editions following notification.

© Derek Pearson 1987

All rights reserved. No part of this publication may be reproduced, stored in a retrieval system or transmitted, in any form or by any means, electronic, mechanical, photocopying, recording or otherwise, without the prior permission of Oxford University Press.

First published 1987
ISBN 0 19 330607 7

Designed by Ann Samuel
Illustrated by Annabel Spenceley

Introduction

This book is a resource collection of songs, poems, games and activities intended principally for the class teacher, occupational therapist, voluntary worker, nurse and parent involved in special education. The material is, however, not limited to special education but could be used equally effectively in the remedial field or in ordinary primary schools. Material from the book has also been used very successfully in play groups, residential homes and schools, and old people's homes and clubs. The only question that needs to be asked is 'does the tune fit the group' in content and sophistication? Much of the material is a working out in full of songs and games mentioned or in extract form in *Hearts, Hands and Voices* and *Sing a Rainbow* by David Ward, and *They can make Music* by Philip Bailey, published by Oxford University Press. References have been made to these books in the text. *Sing a Rainbow* and *Hearts, Hands and Voices* provide a very full and informative background study to the material contained herein and suggestions for further work. (Both *Hearts, Hands and Voices* and *Sing a Rainbow* are now unfortunately out of print but copies should be easily obtainable from libraries.)

Any person with an enthusiasm for music and a basic ability on the guitar can use this book. It is not the concert performance that matters but the pleasure you can experience and pass on to other people. Music reaches everyone and can be an invaluable key to children with special needs. Maximum involvement of the children is of prime importance. There are, for instance, many wheelchair-bound youngsters who can play the guitar parts without much difficulty and derive great satisfaction from being able to lead in their own right. They may not hold the guitar in the traditional 'classical' manner, but, as Philip Bailey has shown, there is usually a way, and the child comes first.

Music is also an aid to language development. Children can be encouraged to discuss and describe or portray in pictures, poems and stories some experience they have shared, e.g. a walk along the sea-shore; a visit to the country, perhaps to a farm, a factory, a supermarket, airport, rail and bus station, etc. By teaching them to improvise around sounds and by judicious provision of words and other materials, you can expand their horizons. This can start at a very simple level with sound games.

The songs have been grouped in five broadly based areas. In each section there are various subsections, usually starting with a song which is then amplified with poems, activities, etc. As you use material from each one the possibility of adding to it and thereby extending the experience of the children will be apparent. This is of particular value as your additions can make the specific reinforcements necessary for your particular children. Never hesitate to change words, add extra verses, change actions, etc., in the songs if it will increase their scope. While the material is grouped into sections this is not meant to restrict its use to that area only. Many of the items can move from section to section and the songs in particular, with a change of words, can assume an entirely new role. Often the introductions to the songs follow a standard pattern, thereby acting as a 'sound signal' for the children to know when to start singing.

Everyone can make music and derive pleasure and a sense of achievement from it. The very act of playing in a group, no matter how simple the level, is a satisfying and enjoyable activity. With children who have behavioural or educational problems this can help towards their ability to work and live with their peers and society in general. So much is learnt in the process: how to hold and play instruments correctly; how to fit their part in with the group, involving listening and counting; when to play and when not to play. All this helps the children to learn the self-control so vital in their general development. Too often we underestimate the ability of those we are working with. Lead them to sing and play musically, and you have given them a source of pleasure and satisfaction for life.

DEREK PEARSON

Accompaniments

The guitar

For guitarists there is a choice of a) playing the part which is written out in full staff notation, b) using the rhythm box and guitar chords indicated above the melody line to make up a simpler accompaniment, c) making up your own style of accompaniment entirely using only the guitar chords indicated.

a) Most of the accompaniments in staff notation suggest using alternative bass notes for some of the chords. This adds interest to the sound of the accompaniment and once you are familiar with the bass notes which can be used with each chord, it is fairly easy to do. The bass notes you will be playing will always fall on the three lowest-sounding strings of the guitar (E A D), while the rest of the chord will be played on the three remaining strings (G B E). These upper notes of the chord can either be strummed with the back of the RH index finger, or plucked by the index (*i*), middle (*m*) and ring (*a*) fingers, as follows:

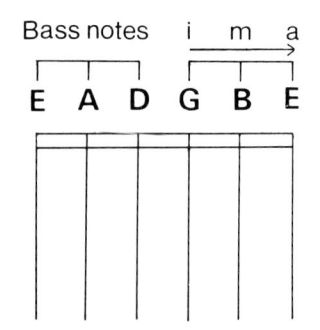

Bass notes   *i*   *m*   *a*

E   A   D   G   B   E

– pluck together or separately or
– strum in direction of arrow

The bass notes you will be using will be the primary bass note which is always the tonic of the chord (i.e. in the chord of D it is the note D), and the secondary bass note which is most often the fifth of the chord (dominant); in the chord of D it is the note A. The third of the chord can also be used as a secondary bass note but in this book it is only suggested in the chord of G, where it is the note B.

Here are the chords you will need to play. They are shown in chord windows and in staff notation and their primary and secondary bass notes are indicated:

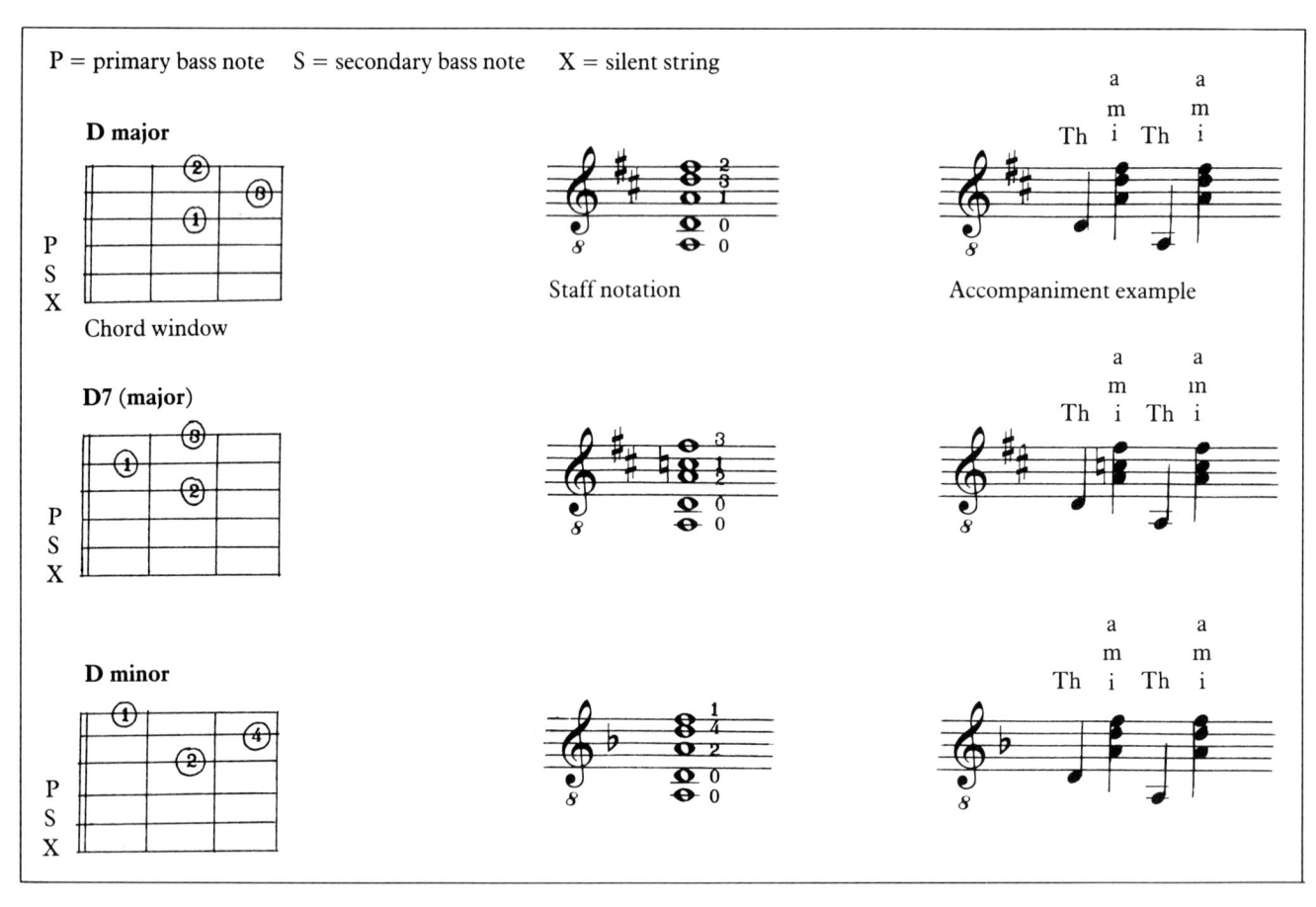

P = primary bass note   S = secondary bass note   X = silent string

D major

Chord window   Staff notation   Accompaniment example

D7 (major)

D minor

A major

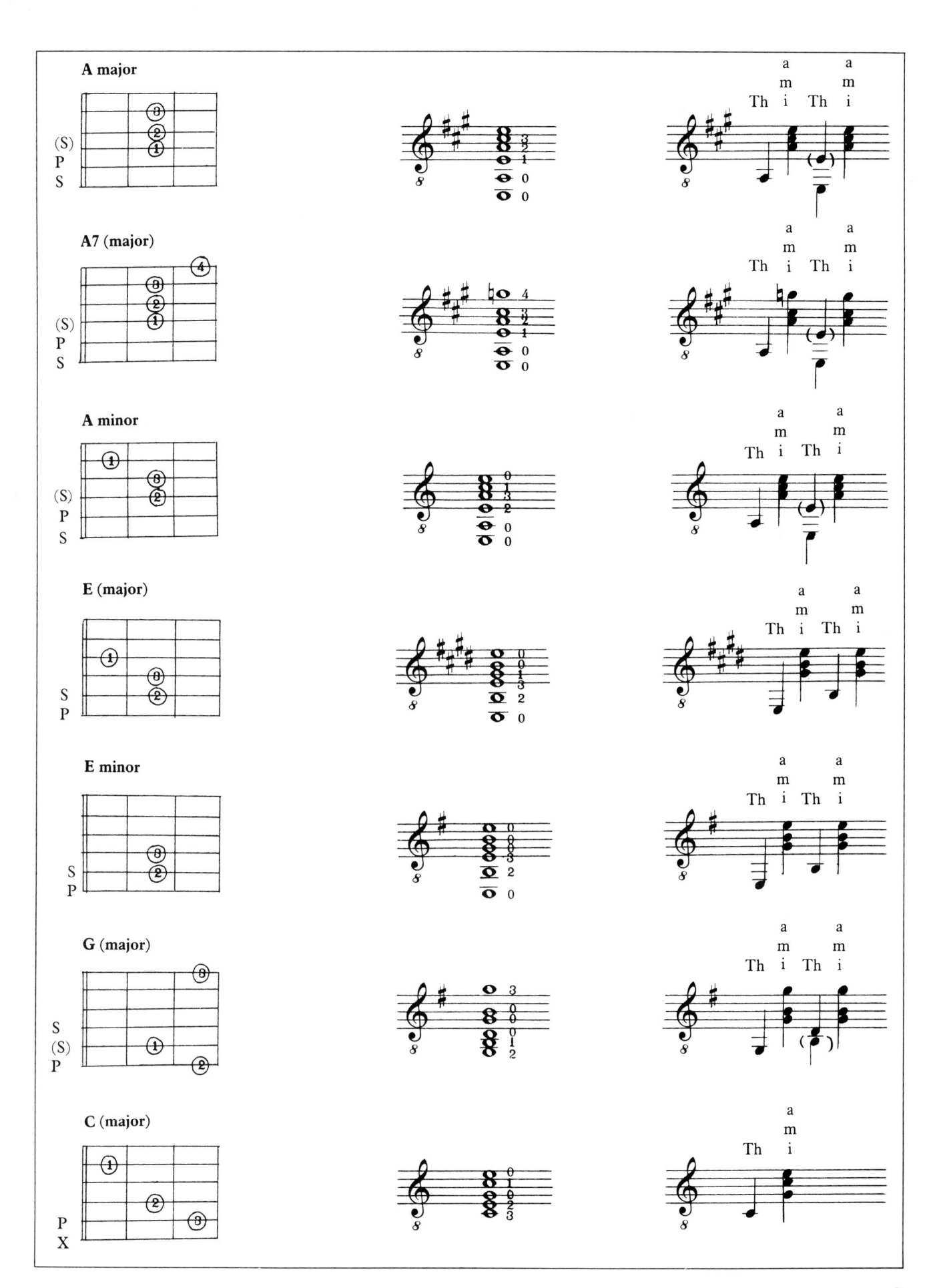

A7 (major)

A minor

E (major)

E minor

G (major)

C (major)

5

B7 (major)

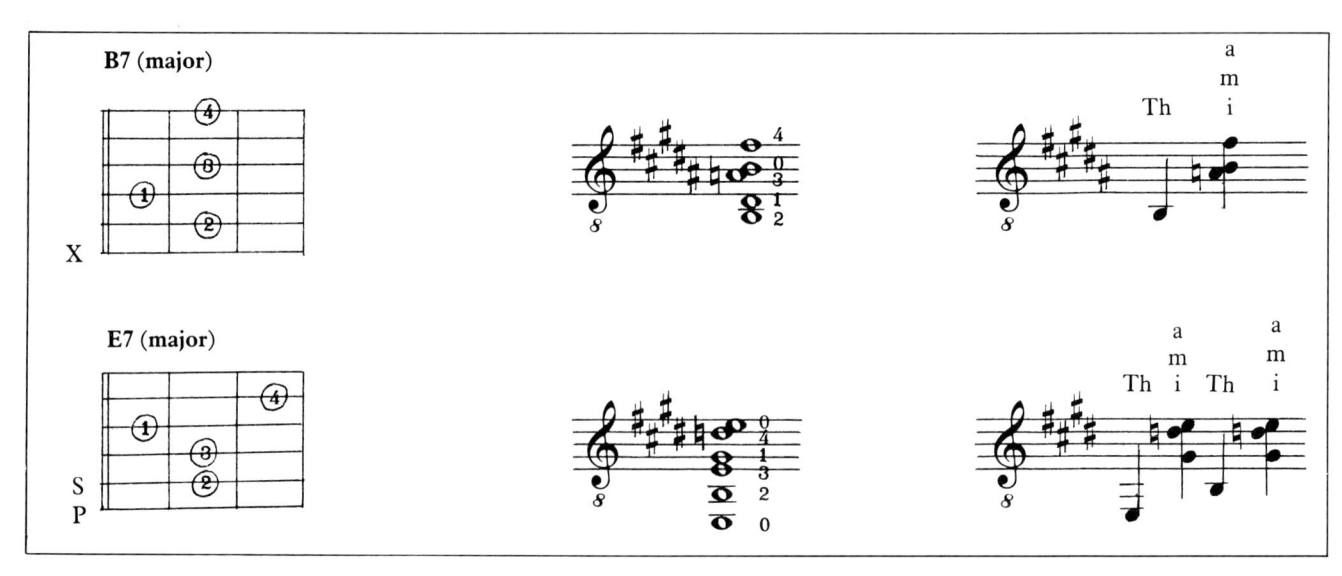

E7 (major)

b) If you find difficulty with reading staff notation but are not familiar enough with right-hand finger styles to devise you own accompaniments, you may find the following suggestion helpful.

Below each song is given a box containing a rhythm and right-hand fingering, e.g.

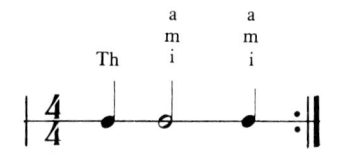

You can use this rhythm and right-hand fingering throughout the song changing position only where the chord above and the melody line changes — and then all you need to change in the right-hand is the bass note which the thumb plays.

Where you see *Th* indicated, play the bass note of the chord with your right-hand thumb (see the chord windows given above) To start with play only the primary bass notes.

Where *i* is indicated, pluck the G string (string 3) with your index finger. Where *m* is indicated, pluck the B string (string 2) with your middle finger. Where *a* is indicated, pluck the high E string (string 1) with your ring finger. When all three are indicated one above the other ᵃ pluck all three strings together. Pluck them
    ᵐ
    ⁱ
separately when they are indicated separately, e.g.

As you gain confidence you will be able to elaborate your accompaniments by alternating bass notes as in the part given in staff notation. Use the chord windows and explanation given above to guide you, and use your ear to tell you whether to play a primary or secondary bass note where *Th* is indicated.

If you prefer to strum rather than pluck an accompaniment, simply strum across all the strings in the chord in the rhythm indicated in the box. Alternatively, play bass notes with your thumb where *Th* is indicated and strum the G, B and high E strings with the back of your index finger where *i*, *m* and *a* are indicated.

This sign ⅗ is usually given at the end of a song and indicates that all the notes of the chord should be strummed with the thumb as a finale to the accompaniment. In one or two songs this style is indicated throughout.

Simple rhythmic variations on the given accompaniments are possible and desirable to add interest, e.g. 'The cabbage patch':

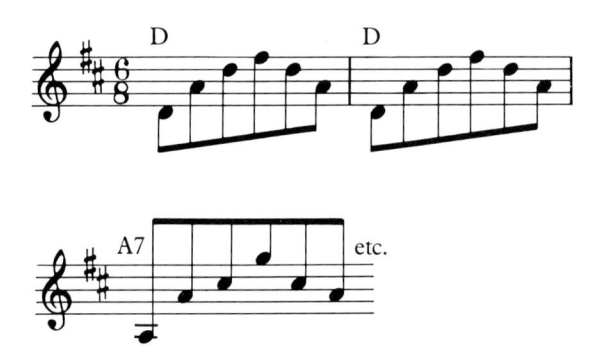

As before, familiarity with the material and simple experimenting will suggest variations in a number of songs. Never allow the variation to obscure the simple harmonic structure of the accompaniment or to upset the rhythmic strength of a song.

Chime bars

Throughout the book parts for chime bars have been added to many of the songs. For 'chime bars' you could read glockenspiels, xylophones and metallophones. If these instruments are available and the particular sound quality of one suits a song then use it. The layout of the bars would be the same in all cases and this is illustrated with each song in which they are used.

Chime bar parts have been written very simply. In many cases the lower note of the chord could be played alone to make an even simpler part. It is possible to lay out the chime bars so that the part can be played as a pattern consisting only of the moves IN and OUT, e.g.

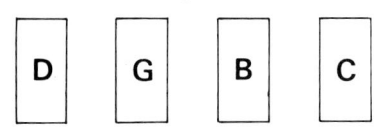

| D | G | B | C |

Play the INner notes G and B and the OUTer notes D and C as pairs. The pattern could be written thus:

| IN | OUT | IN | IN |

A good way to practise this is for a large group to use their hands on their knees. Gently tap on the knees for IN and to the outsides of the knees (in the air) for the OUT. Then when the individuals come to play it on the bars it is much easier.

The bars could also be 'colour-coded' if this were felt to be a help towards identification, e.g.

| D | G | B | C | | IN | OUT | IN | IN |

There is no international standard colour-coding, so any colours can be substituted. However, once you have chosen a set, stick to them. I find strong colours are best. Red, blue and green will cover most of the tunes at the start as you seldom need more than three chords. I try to keep red for 'doh' or the 'home' chord (key chord) in all keys.

Piano

It would be easy for someone who plays the piano a little to adapt the guitar part for use on the piano. Play the melody at the written pitch and play an adaptation of the guitar accompaniment an octave LOWER. This is a simple procedure and with little practice can be used with ease and success.

Auto-harp/chromaharp

The auto-harp can provide an instant accompaniment to any song. Play the guitar chords as indicated by pressing the appropriate button and run a plectrum or the finger nails over the strings. Sometimes it may be appropriate to play the chord twice in the bar to maintain the rhythmic flow, especially in those songs where there are some bars with two different chords and others with only one. Experience will very quickly guide you into what feels and sounds correct.

Should you find that the chords you want are not all available, this is usually easily solved. For example, in the key of A the three most common chords are A, D and E7. Strangely, 'A' is often not available (different manufacturers give different selections of chords). In this case (remembering that only the first seven alphabet names are used in music) move back one letter in the alphabet (i.e. A becomes G, D becomes C, and E7 becomes D7). Now sing in the new key accompanied by the harp. If you wish to use other pitched instruments in the new key, corresponding adjustments have to be made to their parts.

The 15-bar auto-harp is probably the most useful and readily obtainable. It is not too expensive and it is better to pay the extra for the flexibility this provides over models with fewer bars. It is vitally important to keep the auto-harp in tune. Like the guitar it quickly goes out of tune when new, but soon settles down if regularly tuned. This requires a little effort, but is easily repaid in the pleasure it gives the children.

Descant recorder

Many of the melodies of the songs can be played on a descant recorder. Quite a number have been indicated and others are possible but have not been listed mainly because of rhythmic/fingering difficulties. Some are not possible, usually because they go too low for the descant recorder.

Tuned/untuned percussion

Music should start simply, be something in which children can grow and the music grow with them. Never introduce tuned or untuned percussion work until the song itself is secure. The percussion parts can be practised on their own or as a game, then when secure you can put the song and percussion together.

LET'S GO

The realization of one's self is all important in mental and physical health. This can begin with the recognition that eyes, ears, arms, legs etc. are all a part of 'me'. This recognition is an important phase in a child's development, linked closely with things 'I' can do, know and like. Allied with the physical development of motor and muscular control and the associated increase in co-ordination, this helps to develop self-control and a sense of rhythm essential in the refinement of motor skills. Many of the songs in this section allow for simple repetitive movements. The words, melodies and rhythms are simple and strong to enable the children to grasp the idea and succeed where at all possible. Throughout this and all the sections every opportunity should be taken to increase the children's verbal skills. You cannot build without bricks, and words and phrases are the 'bricks' of sentences, stories and language in general.

Let's all sing a happy song   9
Sally go round the sun   10
Hot potato   12
Ha, ha, this a-way   14
Heads and shoulders, knees and toes   16
Walking to the town   18
Right hand, left hand   20
I'm a little Dutch girl   24
Let everyone clap hands like me   26
One finger, one thumb   28
I went to school   30
The way we learn   34
Slowly, slowly   37
Travelling song   38
Jump in the leaves   40
Round and round the circle   42
Rock my soul   44
Say won't you come along with me   46

Let's all sing a happy song

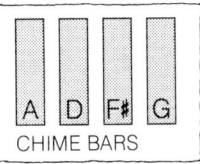

Cheerfully, with good rhythm

Traditional

INTRODUCTION

1. Let's all sing a hap-py song, A hap-py song, a hap-py song. Oh let's all sing a hap-py song Be-cause we're all to-ge-ther.

2 Let's all make a happy sound . . .

Improvise other verses to suit your class or circumstances.

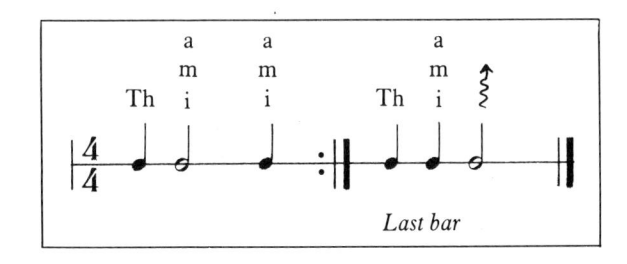

9

Sally go round the sun

Steadily not fast   Traditional

A D CHIME BARS

Sal-ly go round the sun, Sal-ly go round the moon, Sal-ly go round the chim-ney pots, eve-ry af-ter-noon.

Change the name to match those of children in the class. Other verses:

Ian go round the room,
Ian go round the room,
Ian go round the room again

Alan go up the stairs,
Alan go up the stairs,
Alan go up them one by one

Alan go down the stairs . . .

Rhythm change necessary when changing 'every afternoon' to a specific day:

on a Monday afternoon

on a Tuesday afternoon

on a Wednesday afternoon

On a Thursday afternoon.

On a Friday afternoon.

The chime bar part can be practised by taking the right knee as 'D' and the left knee as 'A'. Gently tap each knee with the respective hands, singing the notes 'D' and 'A'. Some of the class could do this while the rest sing the melody. Then the children can take turns to play the chime bar part while the rest sing the song.

The chime bar part is better played an octave lower than written. For this the low pitch chime bars are essential for the note 'A'.

For an Introduction use bars 1 and 2 played twice.

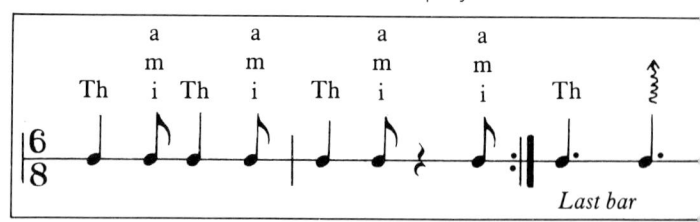

Last bar

10

Movement to drum rhythms

In 'follow my leader' style take a large tambour and play, with a good steady beat, at walking pace. You walk around the available space, the children listening and joining in. The pace can be varied and the beats made louder and softer to maintain attention. When you stop playing everyone stops moving. This is an important idea and the ability to stop and start, as directed, needs practise. There is real benefit in this game. Running, jumping, skipping etc. can also be incorporated. The rhythms will be varied to suit the actions. When playing the tambour, sometimes use a beater. Using your hand, however, gives the possibility of many varied rhythms and sounds that you could not make using a beater; try drumming quickly and firmly from little finger to thumb (really hit hard with the thumb). This can sound very military. Running your finger nails all over the tambour's surface makes a scratchy, swishing sound that is quite eerie. Experiment to find others.

Sound mobile

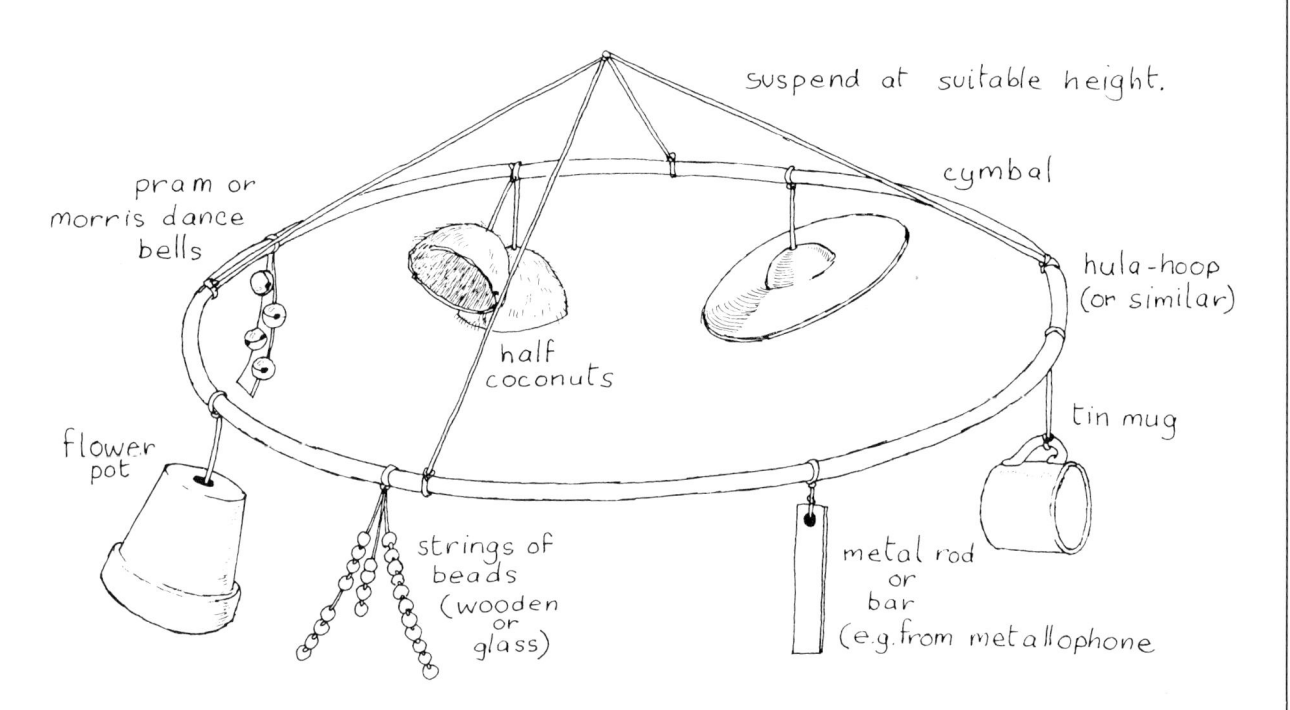

Labels on mobile: suspend at suitable height; cymbal; hula-hoop (or similar); tin mug; metal rod or bar (e.g. from metallophone); strings of beads (wooden or glass); flower pot; half coconuts; pram or morris dance bells.

Many other sound sources can be added to, or substituted for, those on the mobile. Experiment to see how many different kinds of sound you can make by shaking or by tapping the different objects with different kinds of beater. What are the sounds like? Are they loud or soft? How else can you vary the sounds? Do they suggest any other object or place? Can you play a group of sounds together to suggest a story or picture in sound?

Hot potato

Steady, with strong rhythm

Traditional

INTRODUCTION

Lyrics: Hot po-ta-to pass it on, Hot po-ta-to pass it on, Hot po-ta-to pass it on, Get rid of the hot po-ta-to.

Chime bars: A D

The auto-harp would play the guitar chords as indicated. The chime bar part is better played an octave lower than written. The low pitch bars would be essential for this.

This is a game similar to 'Pass the parcel' with the child who is left holding the 'potato' when the music stops being out. Continue until every child is out.

This song is particularly good for co-ordination, left-right awareness and as a simple action song.

To improve co-ordination, begin with a large ball and gradually decrease the size of the ball and increase the tempo of the music. If you don't want to use a ball, make up a large soft parcel and gradually move to smaller ones. If you stop the music in the middle of the song and 'catch' somebody it is better to go back to the beginning of the song to start again, then everyone knows where they are.

The Introduction could be played twice if required. It could also be altered to the 'pattern' type frequently used: | D A7 | D D ‖

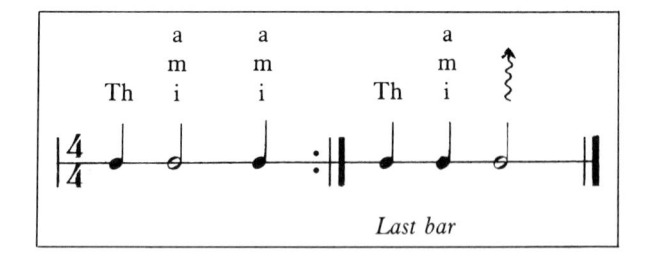

Poetry, language and movement

Poetry like music must be heard. It deals in sound . . . poetry must be read aloud. (*Basil Bunting*.)

When using poems it is often good fun to say them rhythmically. As you say the poem, one half of the class marks the pulse (or beat) while the other half speaks the words, clapping or tapping the rhythm quietly. This can be extended to walking to the pulse, clapping and saying the word-rhythm as you walk. Have a positive direction (e.g. a circle) to move in rather than just anywhere. If you have a large class try two circles, one inside the other, moving in opposite directions. It's interesting!

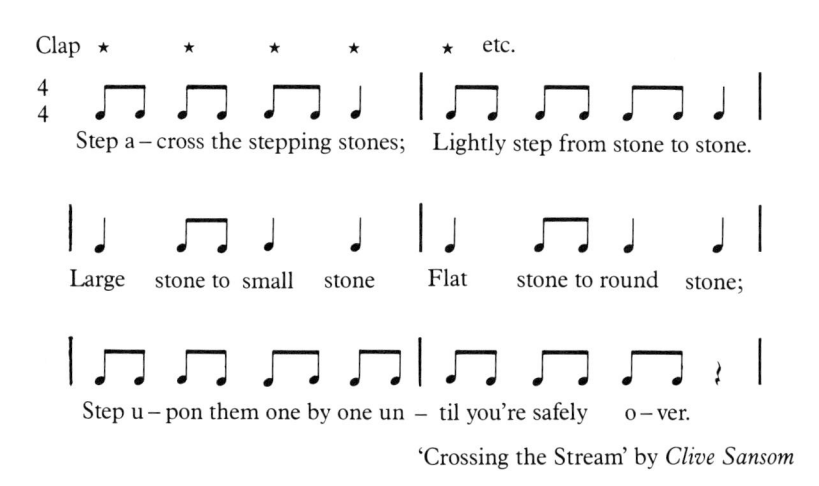

Clap ★   ★   ★   ★   ★ etc.

Step a – cross the stepping stones; Lightly step from stone to stone.

Large stone to small stone   Flat stone to round stone;

Step u – pon them one by one un – til you're safely o – ver.

'Crossing the Stream' by *Clive Sansom*

Mark the pulse by clapping eight times in each line. On the last pulse of the last line 'throw the sound away', on the rest, by moving the hands quickly apart to cover the silent pulse. Always give children something to do on rests.

Juniper, Juniper,

Green in the snow.

Sweetly you smell and

Prickly you grow.

Juniper, Juniper,

Blue in the fall.

Give me some berries,

Prickles and all.

Ha, ha, this a-way

Lively, but not rushed

Huddie Ledbetter

Ha, ha, this a-way, Ha, ha, that a-way, Ha, ha, this a-way, All day long.

1. Now we go marching, marching, marching. Now we go marching all day long.

Other verses (second half only):

2 Now we go walking, walking, walking . . .
3 Now we go skipping, skipping, skipping . . .
4 Now we go hopping, hopping, hopping . . .
5 Now we go running, running, running . . .
6 Now we go jumping jumping, jumping . . .

14

The Introduction may be played twice if it is felt to be too short. You can also play it between the verses.

In the chime bar part the player can

either 1. Count 1 and 2 and 3 and 4 and then start to play the part (to 8 in the case of the Introduction being played twice),

or 2. Play D 4 times, as above, then start to play the part (again to 8 in the case of the Introduction being played twice).

Two beaters should always be used, playing as indicated L=Left Hand, R=Right Hand.

The auto-harp would play the guitar chords as indicated. The chime bar part is better played an octave lower than written. The low pitch bars would be essential for this.

Pocket board

Take a piece of soft-board, 1 cm thick and of length and width to suit your requirements (approx. 75 cm by 100 cm is a manageable size). Using stiff card (2 mm thick) cut enough strips, 10 cm wide, to go from top to bottom with approximately 1 cm overlap. Staple sides and bottom of each pocket to the board using a heavy duty staple gun, starting at the top and overlapping until the foot of the board is reached. If you want to hide the staples, cover with adhesive tape.

Using thin card, make word-cards, phrase-cards, rhythm-cards and picture-cards. They can be made more durable by covering in plastic seal-film. This also enables you to write on them with water-washable overhead projector pens. (A damp cloth or tissue removes the evidence easily for use again next time.)

These cards need to be twice the depth of a board pocket so that they stand clear for reading, writing only on the top half of the card. You can link all the various cards together to reinforce the learning processes for the children.

Pictures can be added, especially with young children, to help associate word, object and the rhythmic structure of the speech. Sometimes there is a slight artificiality in the speech-rhythm, but this is preferable to the lack of rhythmic clarity often found in children's speech, especially those with hearing impairment.

Sunday magazines, glossy magazines, travel brochures, seed catalogues etc. provide sources for pictures that can be used in many subject areas for vocabulary and language enrichment.

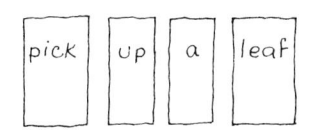

This can be extended to allow the 'build-up' of phrases; pick up a leaf – pick up a *red* leaf – pick up *five green leaves*. The possibilities are endless for simple grammar and sentence construction.

Heads and shoulders, knees and toes

Speed to suit movements

Traditional

A D F# G
CHIME BARS

INTRODUCTION

Heads and shoul – ders, knees and toes, Knees and toes, knees and toes, Heads and shoul – ders, knees and toes, Eyes, ears, mouth and nose.

CHIME BARS

INTRODUCTION

Traditional

Heads, shoul – ders, knees and toes, knees and toes,

CHIME BARS

16

Heads, shoul-ders, knees and toes, knees and toes, — Oh — heads and shoul-ders, knees — and — toes, Eyes, ears and mouth and nose.

The songs can be, and often are, sung unaccompanied in 'follow my leader' fashion. Do the actions suggested in the song with the children.

CHIME BARS: E F# A C# D

Hinges

I'm all made of hinges,
'Cause everything bends;
From the top of my neck,
Way down to my ends.

I've hinges in front
And I've hinges in back,
But I have to have hinges
Or else I would crack.

Helen Fisher

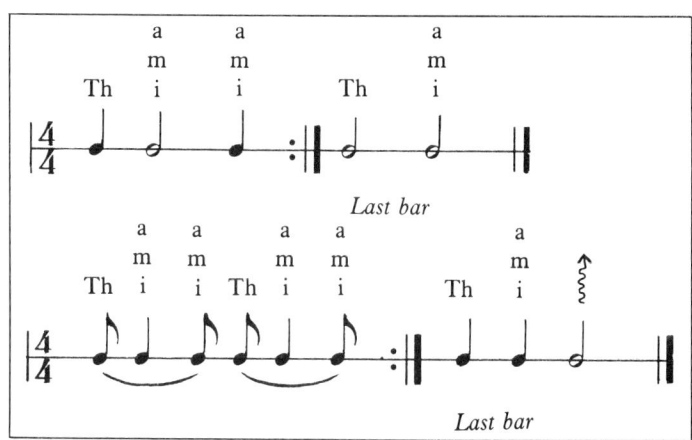

Hands on shoulders

Hands on shoulders, hands on knees,
Hands behind you, if you please;
Touch your shoulders, now your nose,
Now your hair and now your toes;
Hands up high in the air,
Down at your sides and touch your hair;
Hands up high as before,
Now clap your hands, one, two, three, four.

Walking to the town

Speed to suit movements

Tune: traditional
Words: Derek Pearson

INTRODUCTION

2. We're hopping to the town . . .   *Repeat*
3. We're jumping to the town . . .
4. We're crawling to the town . . .   *Repeat*
5. We're running to the town . . .

Alternative verses

We're tired so we'll sit down, (*twice*)
Rest for a little while and then we'll carry on.

We're feeling hungry now, (*twice*)
Let's have some food to eat and then we'll carry on.

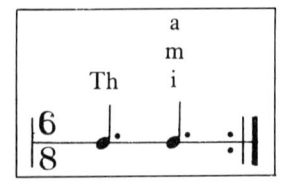

The auto-harp plays two chords to a bar, as indicated, until the second last bar. In this bar play D – A⁷, then D twice in the last bar. This is different from the guitar part but better to sing when using the auto-harp. Vary speed according to activity and ability. Add or omit verses to cover activity range of children. For people without personal mobility the activities could be:

We're driving to the town.	(Steer an imaginary car or bus.)
We're clapping to the town.	(Clap in time to pulse for movement and co-ordination.)
We're whistling to the town.	(Then whistle a verse.)
We're singing to the town.	(Then sing a verse.)

18

Ten miles from home

The tune of 'Walking to the town' is the same as that for 'The farmer's in his den'. Another version of the tune is 'We're ten miles from home'.

> We're ten miles from home, we're ten miles from home,
> We walk a while, we rest a while, we're nine miles from home.

etc. to last verse where the last line is '. . . and now we are home'.

Take large empty cornflake (or similar) packets and cover with plain wallpaper, etc. (Offcuts and odd rolls are often available for little or nothing.) When covered, paint on the numbers 10, 9, 8, etc. to 0. Place them round the room and as you sing the song someone goes and picks up the relevant 'milestone', taking it back to his or her place. Continue until all are collected, then count them, 10, 9, 8, 7, etc. to 0. (See also page 112 in *Out for the count* section.)

After a bath

After my bath
I try, try, try
to wipe myself
Till I'm dry, dry, dry.

Hands to wipe
and fingers and toes
and two wet legs
and a shiny nose.

Just think how much
less time I'd take
if I were a dog
and could shake, shake, shake.

Aileen Fisher

Slowly

Slowly.
Slowly the tide creeps up the sand,
Slowly the shadows cross the land.
Slowly the cart-horse pulls his mile,
Slowly the old man mounts the stile.

Slowly the hands move round the clock,
Slowly the dew dries on the dock.
Slow is the snail – but slowest of all
The green moss spreads on the old brick wall.

James Reeves

Word wheel

Take pieces of card and cut two circles, one 8 cm in diameter, the other 15 cm in diameter. Clip together with a brass-headed paper fastener, the small circle on top of the large one. At the right hand edge of the small circle write the first syllable of a group of words, and round the large circle write the remaining syllables, so that when the circle is rotated it forms these various words (see diagram). It makes a simple language and vocabulary toy that can be duplicated for many groups of words.

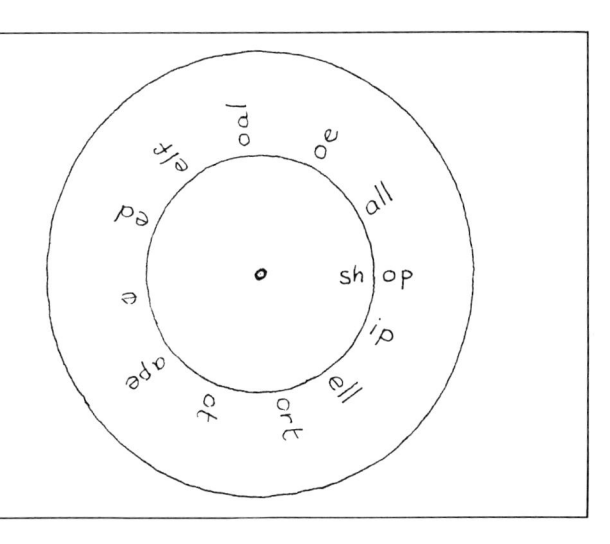

Right hand, left hand

Steady, not fast

Gwen Rosman

INTRODUCTION

This is my right hand, raise it up high. This is my left hand, I'll touch the sky. Right hand, left hand, twirl them a-round. Right hand, left hand, pound, pound, pound. This is my right foot, tap, tap, tap. This is my left foot, tap, tap, tap. Right foot, left foot, dance, dance, dance. Right foot, left foot, dance, dance, dance.

The descant recorder could play the melody.

Last bar

Playing with sound

Blow over the top of an empty lemonade bottle or milk bottle (tall variety). Then fill with some water and blow again. What has happened to the note? Fill more bottles to different levels and produce more notes. Try to tune the notes produced by matching with chime bars. This can be quite tricky and the children will have to listen very carefully. Don't rush it, just take time and you will soon find it becoming easier. You may want to mark the level on the bottles for future use. Can you play some simple tunes on the bottles?

The sound is produced in the same way as a flute produces its sound, by blowing across the sound hole, the bottle opening acting as the sound hole in this case. If you know someone who plays the flute the children would enjoy hearing and seeing one in their own room. Live music is always more interesting and absorbing than recorded sound. Of course, all other instruments would be just as welcome and effective.

Ball games

A lot of language development can be involved in directing, encouraging, and commenting on this fundamental activity.

The size and texture of the balls should vary; large-small, hard-soft, etc. Always describe them verbally for the children and ensure they can experience what you mean so that they can build up the necessary relationships. For some children a large, soft ball made from lightly crushed newspaper tied with string, big and soft enough for them to clutch firmly until they have gained confidence to try different ones, is sufficient. At first it may be enough for them to 'pass' it to each other as they sit, or stand, facing each other, close enough to hand it over. As skill and confidence improve move slowly apart.

As appropriate, involve rolling, throwing, kicking, bouncing, catching, etc. Sometimes make all the movements on the ground, sometimes always in the air. Devise games that involve different types of movement to develop skills: for example, divide the children into teams; put half of each team at one end of the room, and the rest at the other end. The first person must bounce the ball to the other end, then the person there must 'dribble' it back football-style.

Bouncing a ball is very good for co-ordination and to do it rhythmically sharpens up awareness and responses.

BOUNCE	CATCH	BOUNCE	CATCH
John	had	John	had a
Great	Big	Great	Big
Water –	proof	Water –	proof
Boots	on;	Mackin –	tosh and
John	had a	That	said
Great	Big	John	is
Water –	proof	That.	
Hat;			

A.A. Milne

At first bounce the ball standing still. Then move slowly forward and backwards, later walking sideways for four bounces to the right, then back to the left and so on until the poem is complete.

Bounce the ball on the first strong beat in each line. As the lines are very short here there is only one bounce per line. The line structure here has been arranged to keep the points of emphasis clear for the children. It doesn't alter how one would say the poem, just makes it easier for the children to see the pattern. It would be perfectly possible to throw the ball in the air and catch it again to the same rhythmic structure. (See 'One, two, three a-leary', p. 106.)

Songs and rhymes to bounce a ball to

Not fast

Bounce the ball on the ground. Throw it up, bounce it down.

Bounce the ball on the asterisks*

Sing at a speed that allows the children to bounce and catch the ball once in each bar. Repeat as often as necessary. The tune is pentatonic and could have a very simple accompaniment improvised on xylophones, etc. As confidence grows, the children could be encouraged to move as they bounce the ball, forwards, backwards and sideways to left and right (see *The world about us* section).

Christmas candles

One . . Two . . Three –
Help me count the candles
On the Christmas tree.

Four . . Five . . Six –
I'll fix the candles,
You can light the wicks.

Seven . . Eight . . Nine –
In the winter twilight
How beautiful they shine.

Three – times – three:
What a lot of candles
On the Christmas tree!

Counting rhyme

(bounce ball)

Num - ber One	touch your tongue
Num - ber Two	touch your shoe
Num - ber Three	touch your knee
Num - ber Four	touch the floor
Num - ber Five	round the hive (jump and jive)
Num - ber Six	pick up sticks
Num - ber Seven	reach for heaven
Num - ber Eight	jump the gate
Num - ber Nine	pull the line
Num - ber Ten	start a - gain.

As well as being used for ball-bouncing, etc., use this rhyme to mime the suggested actions. Don't rush; speed does not matter, rather have good movements to illustrate the different activities.

Clive Sansom

It ain't gonna rain no more, no more

It ain't gonna rain no more, no more, It
ain't gonna rain no more;
How in the heck can I wash my neck If it
ain't gonna rain no more?

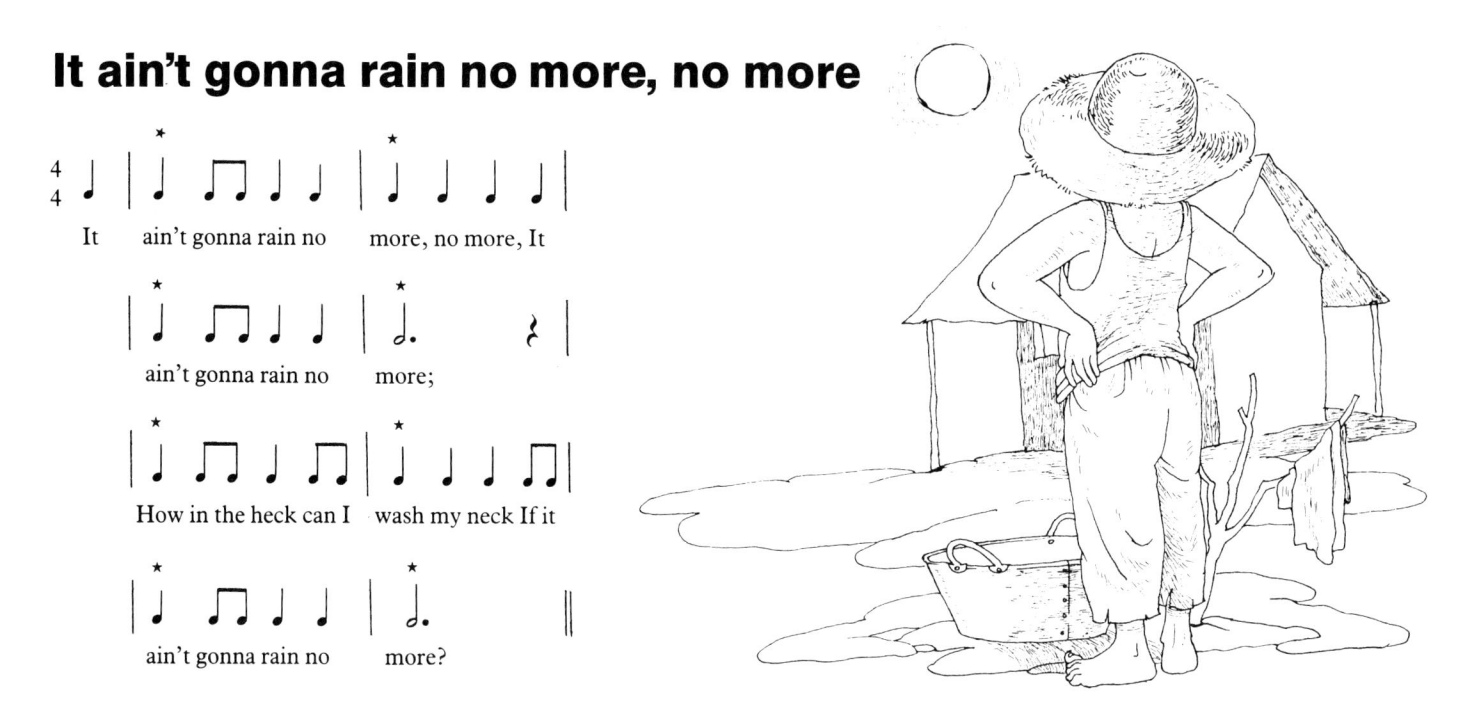

One potato, two potato

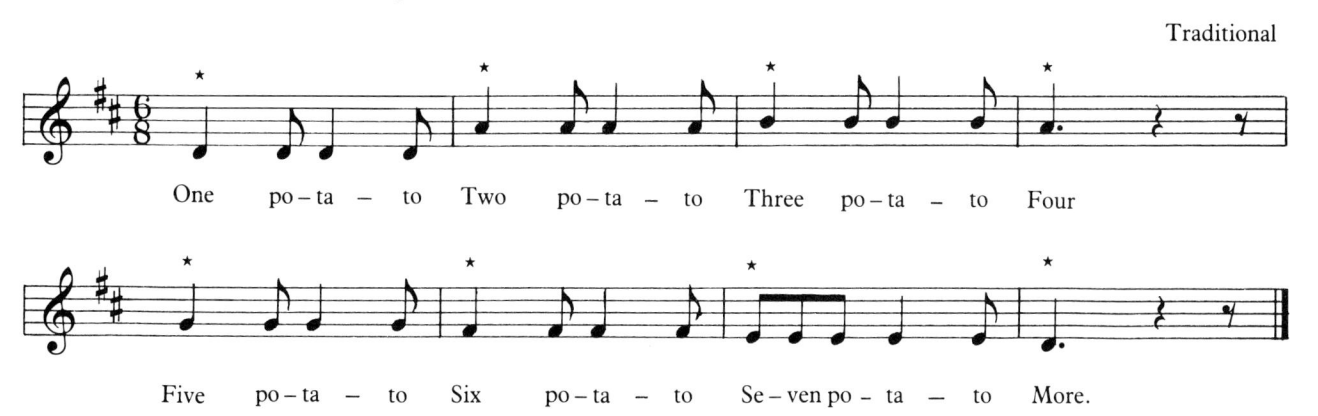

Traditional

One po-ta-to Two po-ta-to Three po-ta-to Four
Five po-ta-to Six po-ta-to Se-ven po-ta-to More.

One, two, three, a-lary,
My first name is Mary.
If you think it necessary,
Look it up in the dictionary.

See each India rubber ball.
Bouncing is not hard at all.
Bouncing, bouncing, bouncing, bouncing.
Bouncing is not hard at all.

(Bounce a ball twice in each line.)

Slowly — to allow for actions

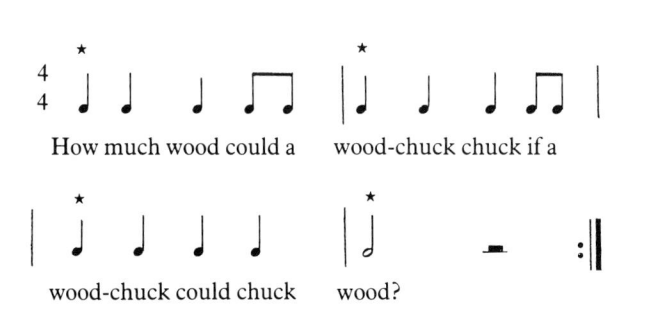

How much wood could a wood-chuck chuck if a
wood-chuck could chuck wood?

Sea-gull sea-gull stay on the sand, It's
always bad weather when you're on the land.

I'm a little Dutch girl

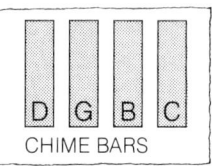

D G B C
CHIME BARS

Speed to suit movements   Traditional

| G | | D7 | G |

1. I'm a lit – tle Dutch girl, Dutch girl, Dutch girl,

| G | | D7 | G |

I'm a lit – tle Dutch girl, Far a – cross the sea.

CHIME BARS

In the chime bar part the lower notes only need to be played for a simple part. The melody can be played on a descant recorder.

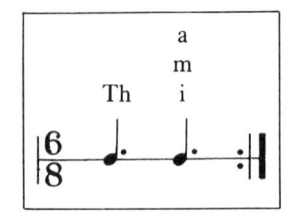

2 I'm a little Dutch boy, Dutch boy, Dutch boy . . .

3 Go away, I hate you, hate you, hate you . . .

4 Why do you hate me, hate me, hate me . . .

5 Because you stole my necklace, necklace, necklace.

6 What colour was it, was it, was it . . .

7 It was a gold one, gold one, gold one . . .

8 Here is your necklace, necklace, necklace . . .

9 Now we're getting married, married, married . . .

24

Follow-my-leader

Follow him up
and follow him down,
Follow him round
and about the town.

Where he will take you to
nobody knows,
But follow your leader
wherever he goes.

Follow him here,
follow him there,
Follow on after him
everywhere.

Where he will take you to
nobody knows,
But follow your leader
wherever he goes.

H. S. Bennett

As well as being used for ball-bouncing this rhyme could be used in the development of the idea of 'concepts'.

Help me wind my ball of wool

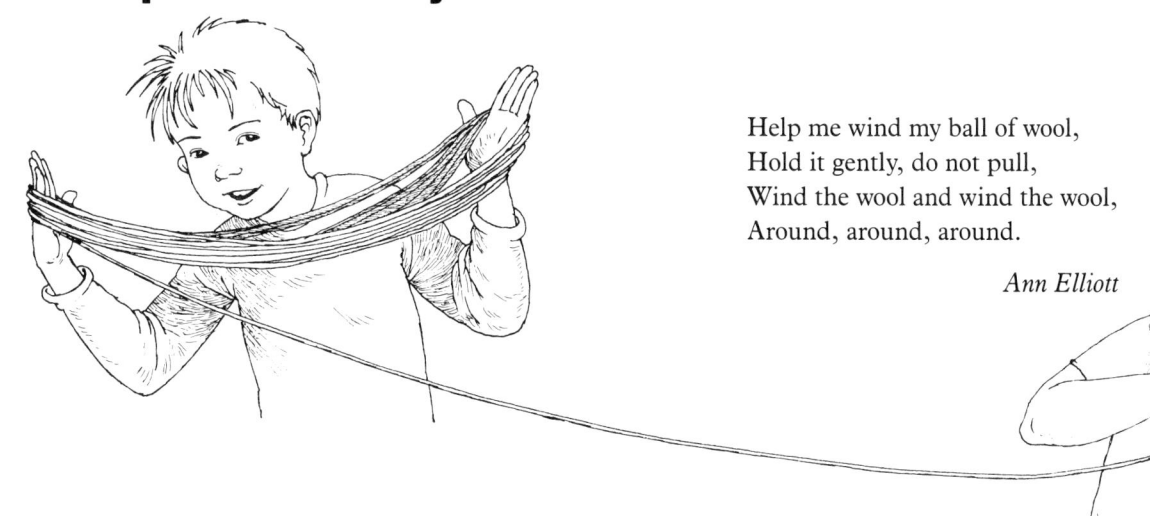

Help me wind my ball of wool,
Hold it gently, do not pull,
Wind the wool and wind the wool,
Around, around, around.

Ann Elliott

Best done in pairs. One holds the wool and the other winds. Co-ordinate the actions.

The tickle rhyme

'Who's that tickling my back?' said the wall.
'Me', said a small
Caterpillar. 'I'm learning
To crawl!'

Ian Serraillier

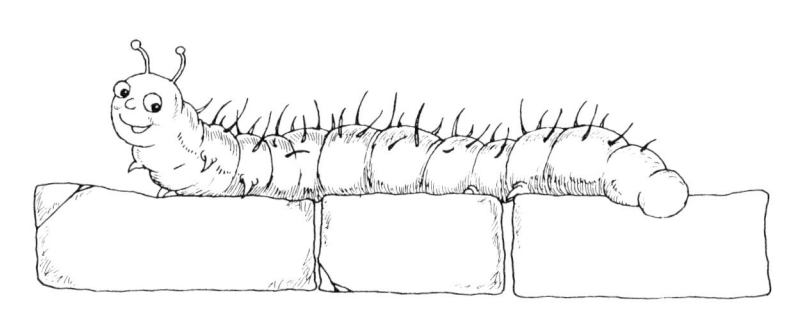

Let everyone clap hands like me

CHIME BARS: A B D F# G

Traditional

Slow waltz
INTRODUCTION

1. Let eve-ry-one clap hands like me, _____ Let eve-ry-one clap hands like me, _____ Come on and join in with the game, _____ Re-mem-ber it's al-ways the same. _____

26

2 Let everyone stamp feet like me . . .
3 Let everyone nod heads like me . . .
4 Let everyone bend down like me . . .
5 Let everyone jump up like me . . .

Make up as many more as you can use.

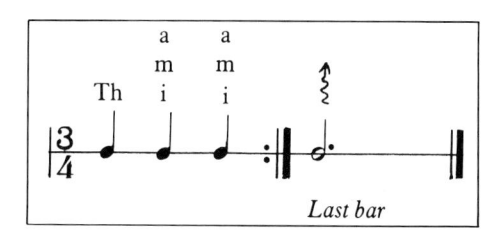

Two little dicky birds

Two little dicky birds
Sitting on a wall
One named Peter
The other named Paul
Fly away Peter
Fly away Paul.
Come back Peter
Come back Paul.

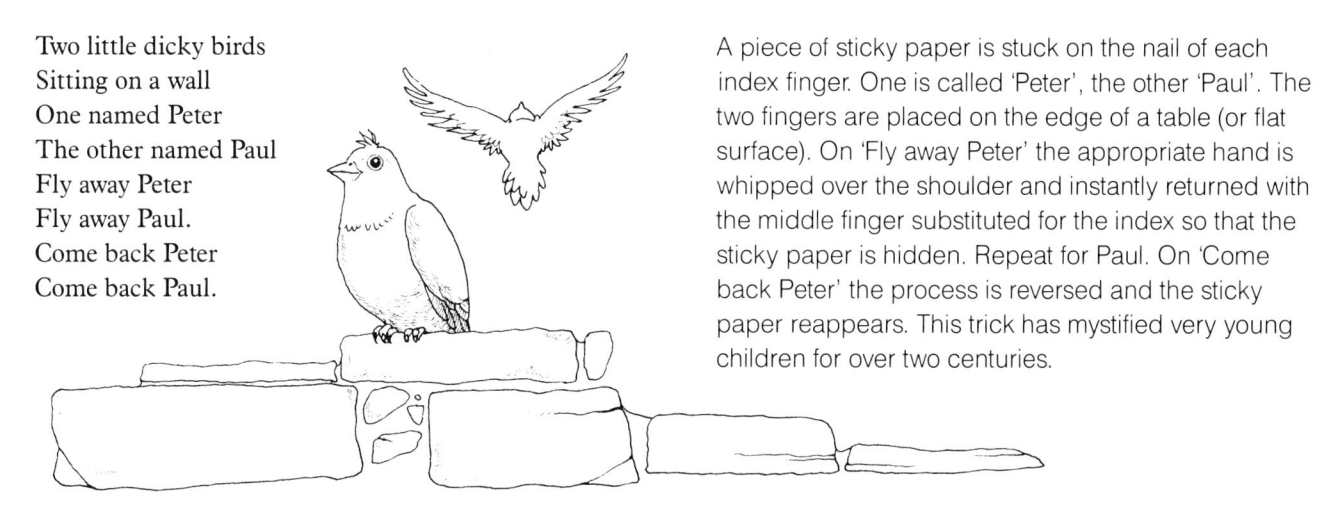

A piece of sticky paper is stuck on the nail of each index finger. One is called 'Peter', the other 'Paul'. The two fingers are placed on the edge of a table (or flat surface). On 'Fly away Peter' the appropriate hand is whipped over the shoulder and instantly returned with the middle finger substituted for the index so that the sticky paper is hidden. Repeat for Paul. On 'Come back Peter' the process is reversed and the sticky paper reappears. This trick has mystified very young children for over two centuries.

Finger rhymes

You twiddle your thumbs and clap your hands,
And then you stamp your feet,
You turn to the left, you turn to the right,
You make your fingers meet.
You make a bridge, you make an arch,
You give another clap.
You wave your hands, you fold your hands,
Then lay them in your lap.

Can you walk on tip-toe
As softly as a cat?
And can you stamp along the road,
Stamp, stamp, just like that?

Can you take some great big strides,
Just like a giant can?
Or walk along so slowly
Like a poor old man?

Sound sensing

All the players (children and adults) sit around the circle with their eyes closed. One person makes a sound using one of the objects. After hearing the sound the others try to reproduce the same sound exactly. Try to ensure that some of the objects have many different ways of producing sound. Later on more than one sound could be used.

One finger, one thumb

CHIME BARS: D G B C

Traditional

Steady, not fast
INTRODUCTION

1. One fin-ger, one thumb, keep mov-ing. One fin-ger, one thumb, keep mov-ing. One fin-ger, one thumb, keep mov-ing. We'll all be hap-py and bright.

2 One finger, one thumb, one foot, keep moving . . .

3 One finger, one thumb, one foot, one elbow, keep moving . . .

4 One finger, one thumb, one foot, one elbow, one head keep moving . . .

Just keep adding parts of the body until the song (and everyone) literally collapses.
(See also *Sing a Rainbow*, p. 15, for suggestions for simple versions.)

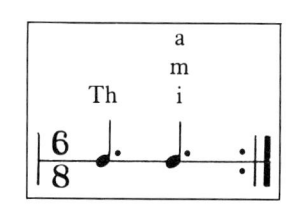

A 'rhyming wall'

Using a Pocket Board (see page 15) build a 'rhyming wall'. Print, in large letters, lots of different words with rhyming sounds. The children each pick a 'brick', read it aloud and, if it 'fits' the particular sound you are using at the time, add it to the wall.

If more than one sound is available to choose from the children will have to select carefully and their discrimination, visual and aural, is improved. (See notes on making board and cards.)

Kim's game

This is a good way to help observation and memory. Place a number of easily identifiable objects on a tray or board and cover them. The number and choice of objects will vary with the age and ability of the children. Gather the children around the tray, ensure each has a clear view, and lift off the cover having told them to look at and remember as many things as they can. Cover the tray after, say, 30 seconds (longer than you think) and see what they can remember. If they can write they should be encouraged to do so to reinforce spelling and vocabulary.

Some possible objects are:
pencil, pen, ruler, notebook, keys, button, coin, spoon, saucer, cup, toothbrush, comb, mirror and anything else appropriate to the ability level of the class.

With young or less able children it could be related to pictures of the objects and flash cards with the words on them to be placed in the pockets of the Reading Frame (see p. 15).

I went to school

Unhurried   Traditional

Chime Bars: A D F# G

INTRODUCTION

1. I went to school one morning and I walked like this, walked like this, walked like this. I went to school one morning and I walked like this, All on my way to school.

Alternative chime bar part

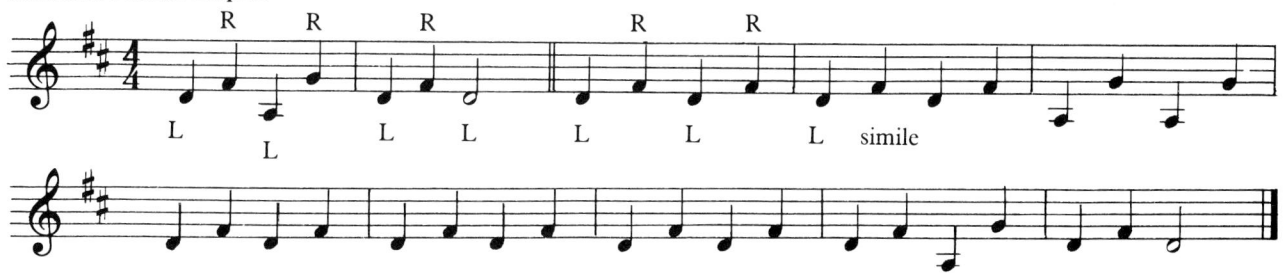

Note: the Introduction and last two bars are the same.

2 I saw a little robin and he hopped like this . . .

3 I saw a little pony and he galloped like this . . .
4 I saw a tall policeman and he stood like this . . .
5 I saw a great big puddle and I splashed like this . . .
6 I heard the school bell ringing and I ran like this . . .

Additional verses

I came to school this morning in a big white bus, etc.
That's how I came to school.

I run around the playground and I jump like this, etc.
Jump all around the school.

I jump into the water and I swim like this, etc.
Swim all around the pool.

Add other verses to suit other activities that the children are involved in. The descant recorder could play the melody. Let clarity of words dictate the speed of the verses.

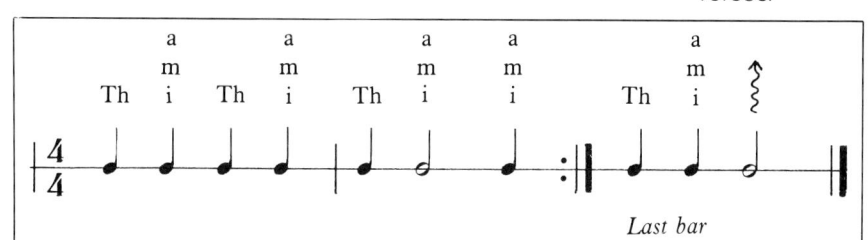

Last bar

Mud

I like mud.
I like it on my clothes.
I like it on my fingers.
I like it in my toes.

Dirt's pretty ordinary
and dust's a dud.
For a really good mess-up
I like mud.

John Smith

Bump

Things that go 'bump!' in the night,
Should not really give one a fright.
It's the hole in each ear,
That lets in the fear,
That and the absence of light!

Spike Milligan

Rainy, rainy, rattle stanes,
Dinna rain on me,
Rain on John O'Groats' house,
Far across the sea.

Rain on the green grass,
And rain on the tree,
Rain on the house top,
But not upon me!

Action games

Mime the chopping of vegetables for soup. The children should say the names of the vegetables they know. With picture, word, and rhythm cards list these and others they do not know. Expand into other areas in which vegetables are used, e.g. salads.

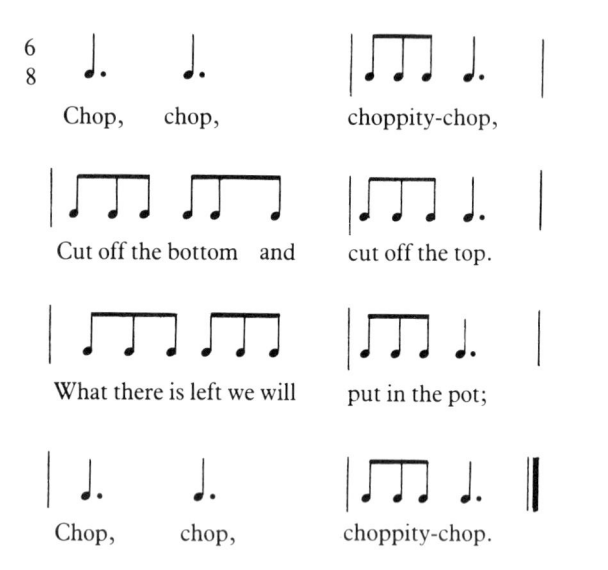

6/8 Chop, chop, choppity-chop,
Cut off the bottom and cut off the top.
What there is left we will put in the pot;
Chop, chop, choppity-chop.

4/4 Celery and apple they are crunchy to eat.
4/4 Grow some cress and eat it.
4/4 Eat lots of grated carrot.

Mime the actions in the poem. On 'slice' and 'spread' take the time given to get all the sounds in. This will also suggest the feeling of spreading and the action of slicing.

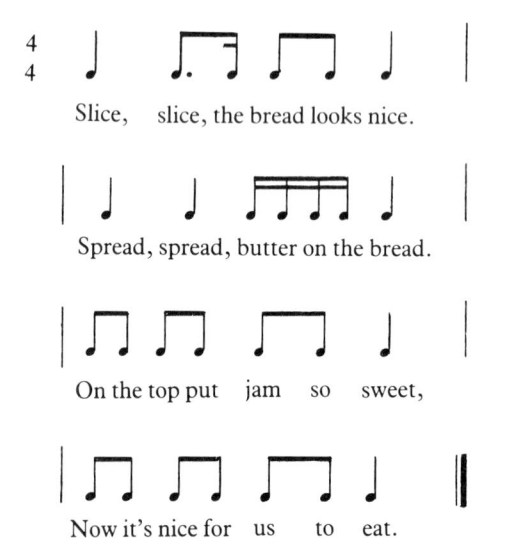

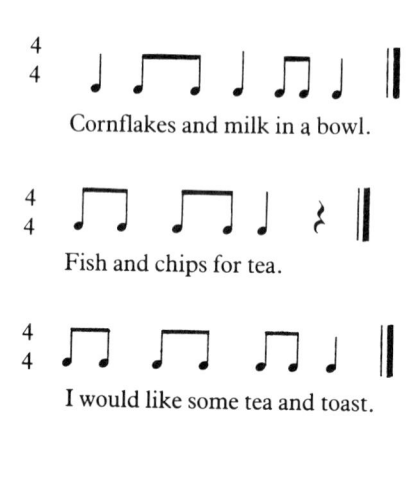

4/4 Slice, slice, the bread looks nice.
Spread, spread, butter on the bread.
On the top put jam so sweet,
Now it's nice for us to eat.

4/4 Cornflakes and milk in a bowl.
4/4 Fish and chips for tea.
4/4 I would like some tea and toast.

Short everyday phrases related to food can be treated in the same way.

A blink

A blink, I think, is the same as a wink,
A blink is a wink that grew,
For a *wink* you blink with only one eye,
And a *blink* you wink with two!

Jacqueline Segal

Noise

Billy is blowing his trumpet;
Bertie is banging a tin;
Betty is crying for Mummy
And Bob has pricked Ben with a pin.
Baby is crying out loudly;
He's out on the lawn in his pram.
I am the only one silent
And I've eaten all of the jam.

Following the music

I stamp my feet
And wiggle my toes
And clap my hands
As the music goes

I reach to the sky
And touch the ground
Up and down to the
Music sound.

I rock to and fro
The way the wind blows;
It's fun to go
Where the music goes.

Hilda I. Rostrom

How many beats?

Teaching the number of beats in a bar to small children is often rather difficult. If you have plenty of room this might help. On the floor either stick five long strips of tape the length of the room, or paint thin lines. These should be 15 cm to 30 cm apart, depending on how long the room is and the floor space available. Have some strips of card or plastic to go from the top line to the bottom line. Cut from stiff card a treble (𝄞) clef. Put this at the left hand end of the lines. Divide the space out with the upright strips and to the right of the treble clef lay a large 2, 3, or 4 cut from card. This is the top number of a time signature. The lower number can come later. The top number tells you the number of beats in a bar. If you have 4 at the start, take some children by the hand and line up next to the 4. Take four steps to each 'bar line', nothing each time you cross an upright line and counting 1 – 2 – 3 – 4 so that when you go from 4 to 1 you cross over a line. Similarly for 2 and 3, etc.

The way we learn

Quite steady

Brenda Piper

INTRODUCTION

1. These are my eyes, These are my eyes, These are my eyes, So I can see.

2 These are my ears . . .
   So I can hear.
3 This is my nose . . .
   So I can smell.
4 This is my tongue . . .
   So I can taste.
5 These are my hands . . .
   So I can feel.

The descant recorder could play the melody.

Last bar

34

Concept charts

Make these charts from large sheets of stiff card on which you stick a number of pictures illustrating the particular idea you wish to put across.

Sounds

The pictures do not need to fit together; they can be irregularly shaped and spaced over the card in 'collage' fashion. Use these cards to start the children talking. What are the objects? What sounds do they make? Which ones are loud? Which ones are soft? Can they think of any other loud and soft sounds?

Using pictures (as suggested, or your own ideas) make up a card to illustrate the idea of loud and soft. Different sizes, and a mixture of loud and soft in the pictures help to maintain the interest.

Senses

Eyes, ears, nose, mouth, hands.

Sight	– reading books, etc.; watching television/films
Hearing	– telephone, music, speech
Smell	– flowers, fresh bread baking, cooker, bonfire
Taste	– licking ice-cream, eating apple
Touch	– feel of fur, sandpaper, etc.; typing, playing violin, etc.

Use pictures to illustrate each sense individually, and one to combine them all. This last picture might well be of a child of similar age to the children you are working with.

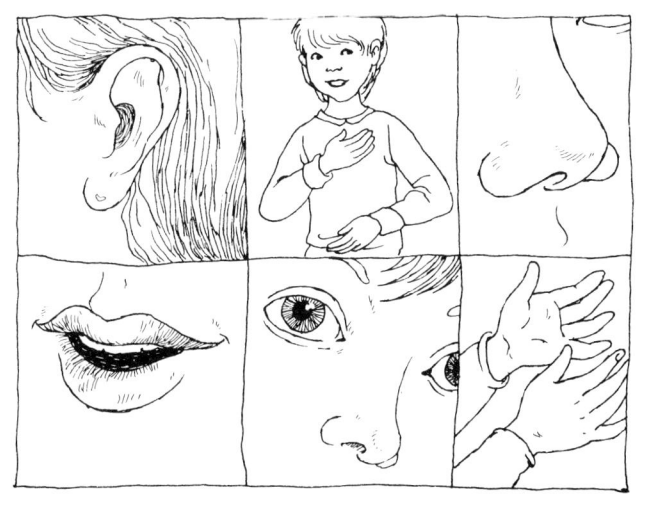

35

More suggestions

Make up other sheets to cover other areas. Adjust the questioning to suit each new area.

Big	**Small**
Elephant	Mouse
Double decker bus	Mini
Large diesel/electric train	Toy train
Gorilla	Baby monkey

(Also horse and foal, mother and newborn baby, hen and chicks, and others.)

Fast	**Slow**
Cheetah or gazelle	Snail
Racing cycle	Invalid chair
Jet aircraft	Stage coach
Power boat	Rowing boat
Q.E.2	*Mayflower*, or other sailing ship
Hare (deer) (use fairy tale)	Tortoise
100 metres runner	Old man with stick

Look also at getting faster/slower.

Up and down	**Left and right**
Ladders, steps, staircase	Road and street signs
Lifts, escalators	Highway code
Climbing hills/mountains	
Ski-ing down hills/mountains (slalom)	
High jump, long jump, show jumping, big dipper at fair.	

You could also include heavy – light, far – near, dark – light (language connection here), happy – sad, etc.

The best sources for pictures are the Sunday supplements, women's glossy magazines, 'National Geographic' or similar magazines, and some trade journals, if these are available. I find it best to collect interesting pictures that I think may be useful, so that when I am making a chart I have an instant source to draw upon.

Make up some charts of pictures with an 'odd one out' using, say, four drawings or pictures: three would be of the same concept and one different. The children should be asked to say which one is different and why. Can they think of any others?

Every opportunity to encourage language development should be taken. The very act of talking and associating sounds with actions, directions, objects and experiences is valuable. It also increases

High and low (Objects)

Tall tree	Mushrooms
Pole vaulter	Limbo dancer
Clouds (in sky)	Grass

High and low in a house (ceiling, floor, chimney – front and back door)
Shoes (flat heels – high heels)
Houses, bungalow – high-rise flats

High and low (Sounds)

Telephone bell	Foghorn
Glockenspiel	Bass xylophone
Small bell (hand type)	Big Ben

Loud and quiet

Road drill	Sewing machine
Large waterfall	Small stream
Shout	Whisper
Lion roaring	Cat purring

Hot and cold

Fire	Ice
Sun	Moon
Soup	Ice-cream
Oven	Refrigerator
Hot desert, e.g. Sahara	Polar Cap

vocabulary, especially as it allows the calculated input of new material by the teacher, suited to the needs of the children.

The following songs in the book reinforce these concepts, as do the poems printed in this section:

Sally go round the sun (p. 10)
Right hand – left hand (p. 20)
I went to school (p. 30)
The way we learn (p. 34)
Slowly, slowly (p. 37)
Rock my soul (p. 44)
Up, up and away (p. 142)
The flying saucer song (p. 112)
The three bears (p. 120)
Incy wincy spider (p. 90)

Slowly, slowly

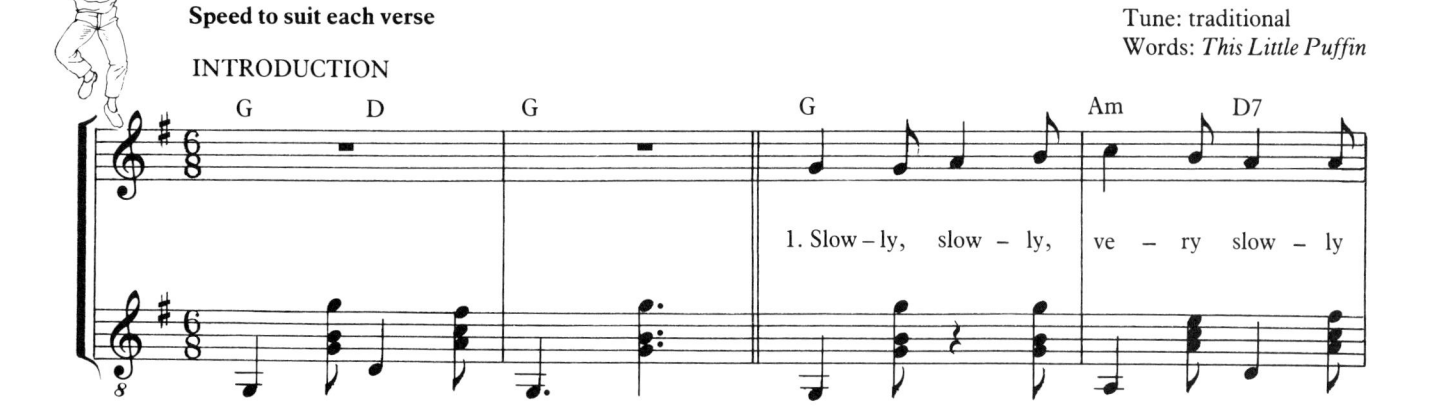

Speed to suit each verse

Tune: traditional
Words: *This Little Puffin*

INTRODUCTION

1. Slow-ly, slow-ly, ve-ry slow-ly creeps, creeps the gar-den snail. Slow-ly, slow-ly, ve-ry slow-ly Up the woo-den rail.

2. Quickly, quickly, very quickly
   Runs, runs the little mouse.
   Quickly, quickly, very quickly
   Round about the house.

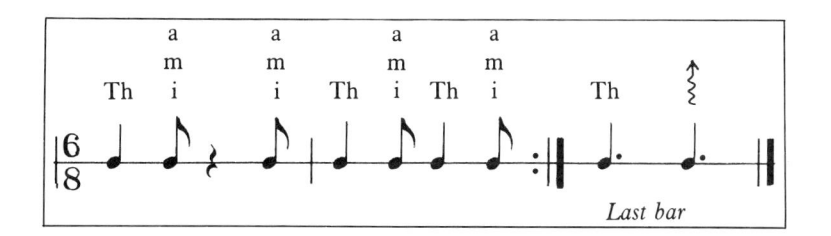

Finger play

Finger and hand mime to suggest or indicate the actions implied in the words. Could also be used for crawling and running.

37

Travelling song

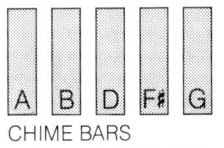

With a swing

Brenda Piper

INTRODUCTION   VERSE

1. When I'm travel-ling, travel-ling a-long, I will sing my hap-py song. La la la la la la la la la, la la la la la la la la la.

INTERLUDE

2. When I'm travelling, travelling along,
   I will whistle my happy song . . .

3. When I'm travelling, travelling along,
   I will hum my happy song . . .

'Travelling, travelling' could be replaced by walking, running, jumping, hopping, etc. and so broaden the scope of the activity. Retain the Interlude but decide whether you are going to whistle or hum during it.

Row, row, row your boat

Row, row, row your boat, gently down the stream,
Merrily, merrily, merrily, merrily, life is but a dream.

Sing the song and take some long poles (broomhandles or similar). Place the children alternately on each side of the pole, and as they sing they 'row the boat'. Sing steadily, 'rowing' the boat on the strong beats with long stretches and pulls on the oars.

The song could be incorporated into a story where people had to get into a boat and row ashore. The words could be changed to suit the situation, e.g.
'Row, row, row your boat, strongly to the shore,
   Pull away, pull away, pull away, pull away, strongly to the shore'.

This could be used as they row ashore to the pirates' island to look for the buried treasure! Discuss with the children and invent stories round simple activities like this.

Row, boys, row

Row, boys, row
As up the river we go.
With a long pull,
And a strong pull,
Row, boys, row.

Clive Sansom

Jump in the leaves

Moderate, with good rhythm
INTRODUCTION

Tune: traditional
Words: Derek Pearson

1. Oh, I love to jump in the leaves, Oh, I love to jump in the leaves, Oh, I love to jump in the leaves. Lets all jump in to—ge—ther.

2. Rake them up to make a big pile . . .
   Let's rake them all together.
3. In the sacks we pack all the leaves . . .
   And take them to make compost.
4. Next year when it's all rotted down . . .
   We'll spread it round the garden.
5. Then we'll watch the plants all grow . . .
   To give us food and flowers.

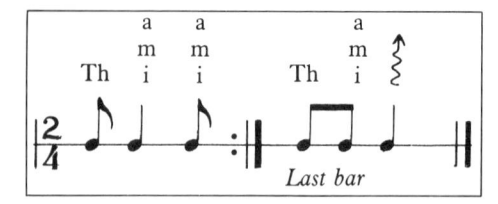

Last bar

In autumn gather a selection of leaves, preferably on a walk through a park or woods with the children. Ask the children to sort the leaves into different colours – red, yellow, brown, green, etc. Why are some leaves green? Why are some trees green all year? Make a leaf collage. Make a tree with leaves for 'all the seasons'. Cut the leaves out from coloured papers of all kinds and stick on to the branches of the tree for that season. Many trees in winter have no leaves – why? What is compost? Is it only leaves that make up compost? Name some of the vegetables and fruits we can grow in the garden and also the flowers. Can you find pictures of them? (Seed catalogues are a good source.)

The descant recorder could play the melody.

A game with trees

Cut a large number of trees from card. The easiest are pine trees:

If the triangles (trees) are cut alternately from a long strip of card and the 'trunk' glued on the back later this saves card.

Green card is best, but you can 'speckle' paint plain card trees by laying them out on sheets of newspaper. Use a green car touch-up spray and spray at an angle from above. Don't attempt to cover the card entirely, just a grading of speckles from top to bottom is sufficient. The trunks can be cut from brown card stiff paper and stuck on the back. A strip of plastic film stuck along the bottom of trees allows you to write words with a water washable O.H.P. pen. When you have finished with one set of words they can be removed with a damp cloth or tissue. A good way to start the game is to use a Pocket Board and 'build' the words with the children, e.g.

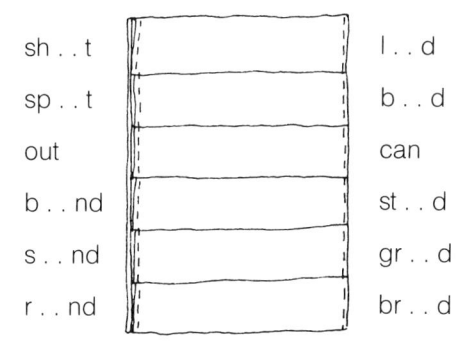

sh . . t	l . . d
sp . . t	b . . d
out	can
b . . nd	st . . d
s . . nd	gr . . d
r . . nd	br . . d

Then write the words on the trees and the children can take turns in adding them to the 'forest'. Stick the trees on to the wall or board using a plastic-type adhesive.

Sweeping

Pick up the broom to sweep the floor,
Sweep the dust carefully out of the door.
Remember the corners and under the mat
And mind where you step as you sweep
past the cat.
Carefully now, sweep the dust to a pile,
Now you can sit and rest for a while.

J. Lambert

Preserving beech leaves

Many leaves can be preserved, both evergreen and deciduous. Beech branches and other deciduous leaves are best cut in late summer just before they colour. Evergreens must be on one year old wood as new leaves are not suitable.

Stand the branches in a narrow container, deep enough to support them. Mix one third glycerine with two thirds boiling water, sufficient to fill the container to about two to three inches, and boil for a minute or so. The branches should be put into the hot mixture and left for several days.

Beech, etc. must be left until the glycerine mixture has spread through all the leaves. Evergreens which turn attractive shades of brown can be removed with some of the original colour remaining. When using them, arrange in vases containing no water.

The best ones to use are beech, maple and similar tough-leaved trees or shrubs in the deciduous varieties, laurel or eucalyptus in the evergreens. You could also use gladioli leaves. Look at the shape, size and colours of leaves. Watch the leaves in different seasons. Look at the size and shape of the trees. Make a tree collage.

To and fro

To and fro, to and fro
Sweeping with my broom I go.
All the fallen leaves I sweep.
I've a big and tidy heap.

Jennifer Day

Beech leaves

In autumn down the beechwood path
The leaves lie thick upon the ground.
It's there I love to kick my way
And hear the crisp and crashing sound.

I am a giant, and my steps
Echo and thunder to the sky.
How the small creatures of the woods
Must quake and cower as I go by!

This brave and merry noise I make
In summer also when I stride
Down by the shining, pebbly sea
And kick the frothing waves aside.

James Reeves

Round and round the circle

CHIME BARS: A B D F# G

Not too fast. Very rhythmical
INTRODUCTION

Traditional

Round and round the cir-cle, Round and round the cir-cle, Round and round the cir-cle, As we have done be-fore.

other versions

Other versions (as 'Alternative chime bar part' overleaf)

1 Round and round the village . . .
  As we have done before.

2 In and out the windows (doorways) . . .
  As we have done before.

3 Take yourself a partner . . .
  As we have done before.

4 Bow before you leave her (him) . . .
  As we have done before.

Possible alternative or extra to verse 4.

Shake hands be – fore you leave her (him) . . .

Also

Keep that wheel a turning . . .
And do a little more each day.

This is the chorus of the song 'William Brown'. Accompaniment for verses of song ‖:D|A7|A7|D:‖ using the same rhythmic structure as above.
Chorus of song as in 'Round and round the circle'.

Actions

Form a circle, join hands with neighbours, arms held high. One child moves 'round the circle' (or village). In verse 2 the child weaves 'in and out', and in verse 3 takes a partner and dances round the circle. In verse 4, first person bows or shakes hands and rejoins the circle, the 'partner' starts the game off again.

Alternative chime bar part

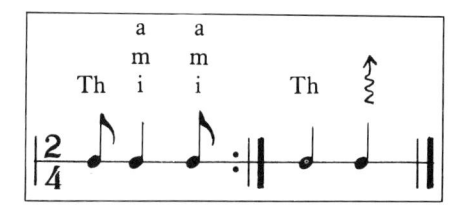

Sink song

Scouring out the porridge pot,
   Round and round and round!

Out with all the scraith and scoopery,
Lift the eely ooly droopery,
Chase the glubbery slubbery gloopery,
   Round and round and round!

Out with all the doleful dithery,
Ladle out the slimy slithery,
Hunt and catch the hithery thithery,
   Round and round and round!

Out with all the obbly gubbly,
On the stove it burns so bubbly,
Use the spoon and use it doubly,
   Round and round and round!

J. A. Lindon

Errantry

There was a merry passenger,
a messenger, a mariner:
he built a gilded gondola
to wander in, and had in her
a load of yellow oranges
and porridge for his provender;
he perfumed her with marjoram
and cardamom and lavender.

J. R. R. Tolkien

Even just the sound of the poem as it is read has a beauty and satisfaction to the ear that children (and adults) find attractive.

At the supermarket

Take the trolley,
   Push it round,
Castor sugar?
   Get a pound.
There's the cocoa,
   Take a tin.
Here's a loaf,
   But it's cut thin.
There's another.
   That will do.
Now we'll find
   Some jam for you.
Choose a jar.
   Yes, strawberry
Will suit your Dad
   And also me.
A tin of fish,
   A bag of rice,
That cream-filled cake
   Looks very nice.
We must have soap
   And toothpaste too,
This green shampoo
   Will do for you.
Apples and pears and
   Two pounds of peas,
A cabbage, a swede
   And a turnip, please.
I nearly forgot
   My jar of honey.
I wonder if we
   Have got enough money?
Push the trolley
   To the till.
I'll fetch a box
   For you to fill.
Leave the empty
   Trolley here.
My purse is empty
   Too, I fear.

Barbara Ireson

Rock my soul

Not too fast

Spiritual

INTRODUCTION

CHIME BARS

1st part

Rock my soul in the bo-som of A-bra-ham, Rock my soul in the bosom of A-bra-ham,

Rock my soul in the bosom of A-bra-ham, Oh, rock my soul.

2nd part

So high I can't get o-ver it, So low I can't get un-der it,

So wide I can't get round it, Oh, rock my soul.

3rd part

Rock my soul, Rock my soul, Rock my soul, Rock my soul.

Last bar

All three parts can be sung together, part 3 over the same accompaniment. Invent actions to suit, particularly the second part. Quiet, rhythmic clapping on the first and third beats of the bar is effective. Those unable to clap could tap on a table or on the floor with a foot.

Say won't you come along with me

Not fast, bouncy rhythm

Tune: Arthur Benjamin
Words: Derek Pearson

CHIME BARS: A D F# G

INTRODUCTION

Say, won't you come a–long with me, we'll go for a walk, We'll go for a walk, we'll go for a walk. Say, won't you come a–long with me, We'll go for a walk, We'll go for a walk to

46

Make up other verses, e.g.

Say, won't you come along with me . . .
We'll go for a swim today.
Ah, now that would be nice . . .
Oh, how I'd like to have a swim.

The chime bar part, apart from the Introduction, can be taught as patterns.

```
         IN   IN   OUT  IN   etc.
Verse    D    D    A7   D    D   D   A7  D
Chorus   A7   D    A7   D    A7  D   A7  D
```

The Introduction can be omitted on the chime bars if it is going to cause dificulties. Rather leave it until later, when confidence has grown. Then put it in to finish off the piece.

This could be played on maracas throughout. Teach it by saying it aloud rhythmically. Everyone could practise it by gently tapping the rhythms on the correct knees with the respective hands. The pattern alternates starting first with the left hand, then with the right. This is quite tricky and really makes people think. It is good for co-ordination. If the rhythms are practised this way as a game, when you give someone the maracas it is much easier to establish them in the context of the song.

The snail

Search round in the garden,
You're bound to find a snail.
Perhaps you've always wondered why
They leave a sticky trail?
Some people think its left for friends
To show which way they're going.
Well, that's not the reason that
A snail leaves a trail showing.
The answer's plain. They cannot see
An inch beyond their noses.
Or recognize the rockery
From a bed of roses.
And snails have no memory
Which gets them in a mess.
That's why they wear their houses,
To remember their address.
And so they leave a sticky trail,
Strange as it may seem.
Not to show the way they've gone,
It's to remind them where they've been.

Jeremy Lloyd

Frogs jump

Frogs jump
Caterpillars hump

Worms wiggle
Bugs jiggle

Rabbits hop
Horses clop

Snakes slide
Seagulls glide

Mice creep
Deer leap

Puppies bounce
Kittens pounce

Lions stalk
But I walk.

Upside down

It's funny how beetles
and creatures like that
can walk upside down
as well as walk flat:

They crawl on a ceiling
and climb on a wall
without any practice
or trouble at all,

While I have been trying
for a year (maybe more)
and still I can't stand
with my head on the floor.

Aileen Fisher

Sound stories

Where possible take a story, or a poem and create sounds to illustrate the atmosphere, events, happenings, location, time, etc. Use natural vocal and body sounds, environmental sounds, those created on tuned and untuned percussion and other available instruments. Encourage discussion about which sounds suit the text and whether or not it is possible to improve on first thoughts. This can be valuable in promoting real listening, not just passive hearing. Start with something short and simple that only needs a few sounds to establish the idea, for example 'Mr Tortoise'.

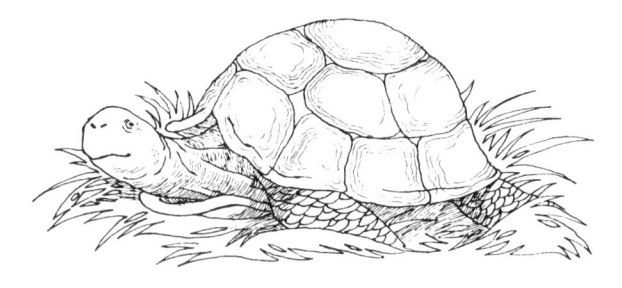

Mr tortoise
Someone is stirring in his nest of hay.
   (*gentle crushing and rustling of newspaper*)
Someone pushes soft soil and dead leaves away.
   (*more newspaper – rub hands over desk or table tops*)
Up into the sunshine comes a little nose,
   (*gentle tap, with a soft-headed beater, on large suspended cymbal on the word 'sunshine'; sounds as in previous line; stop on the cymbal sound*)
Off into the garden Mr Tortoise goes.
   (*gentle tap with soft-headed beater on a low pitch drum, or very quiet taps with the flat palms of hands on desks or tables*)

These sounds are only suggestions. You, or the children, can probably think of many more sounds to create your own special sound picture.

Other stories that can be used in this way are 'The hairy toe' (p. 85), 'Three billy goats Gruff' and 'The gingerbread boy'.

TIME FLIES

For many children, the appreciation of the basic elements of 'time' in relation to their lives and the 'special occasions' that occur during the course of a year needs to be developed, or at least reinforced. 'Special days' and holidays can be helpful in learning the months and the seasonal divisions of the year. This idea can be somewhat abstract and a problem for children with learning difficulties to assimilate. However, in a frame of reference centred round the seasons and the 'events' contained within them, it becomes meaningful. They can look forward with anticipation to autumn with Harvest and Hallowe'en; winter with Christmas and St. Valentine's Day; spring with Easter and April Fool's Day, etc.

An understanding of time helps to give a sense of routine and stability. It provides things to talk about, sing about, opportunities to make things, dramatize and celebrate.

Don't forget the children's own birthdays, probably one of the most important times of the year for them.

Days of the week   *51*
A Valentine song   *52*
Happy Birthday   *54*
The seasons   *56*
April Fool   *58*
Everybody loves Saturday night   *60*
Pray God bless/Round the seasons   *62*
A name carol   *65*
Christmas   *67*
Hear the glad tidings   *68*
Nature carol   *70*

The world is day-breaking

The world is day-breaking!
The world is day-breaking!

Day arises
From its sleep.
Day wakes up
With the dawning light.

The world is day-breaking!
The world is day-breaking!

What are days for?
Days are where we live.
They come, they wake us
Time and time over.
They are to be happy in:
Where can we live but days?

The world is day-breaking!
The world is day-breaking!

Sekiyo Miyoshi

Good morning when it's morning

Good morning when it's morning
Good night when it is night
Good evening when it's dark out
Good day when it is light
Good morning to the sunshine
Good evening to the sky
And when it's time to go away
Good-bye
Good-bye
Good-bye.

Mary Ann Hoberman

Busy day

Pop in
Pop out
Pop over the road
Pop out for a walk
Pop in for a talk
Pop down to the shop
can't stop
got to pop

got to pop?

pop where?
pop what?

well
I've got to
pop round
pop up
pop in to town
pop out and see
pop in for tea
pop down to the shop
can't stop
got to pop

got to pop?

pop where?
pop what?

well
I've got to
pop in
pop out
pop over the road
pop out for a walk
pop in for a talk . . .

Michael Rosen

Time to get up

A birdie with a yellow bill
Hopped upon the window sill,
Cocked his shining eye and said:
'Ain't you 'shamed, you sleepy head?'

Robert Louis Stevenson

Hello's a handy word

Hello's a handy word to say
At least a hundred times a day.
Without Hello what would I do
Whenever I bumped into you?
Without Hello where would you be
Whenever you bumped into me?
Hello's handy word to know.
Hello Hello Hello Hello.

Mary Ann Hoberman

Fork week

You're going to lay the table.
You go to the drawer to get the knives, forks and spoons.
You find the forks
You find the spoons
but the knives – they've all gone.
You look everywhere
the sink, the table, the draining board
but they've all gone.

A few days later – it's the same
only it's the spoons this time
and all the knives have come back.

My brother,
he's worked it out,
he says they take it in turns to disappear.
'It's alright,' he says,
'We won't see another fork till Thursday,
it's Fork Week.'

Michael Rosen

Days of the week

Moderate
INTRODUCTION

W.E. Stiles

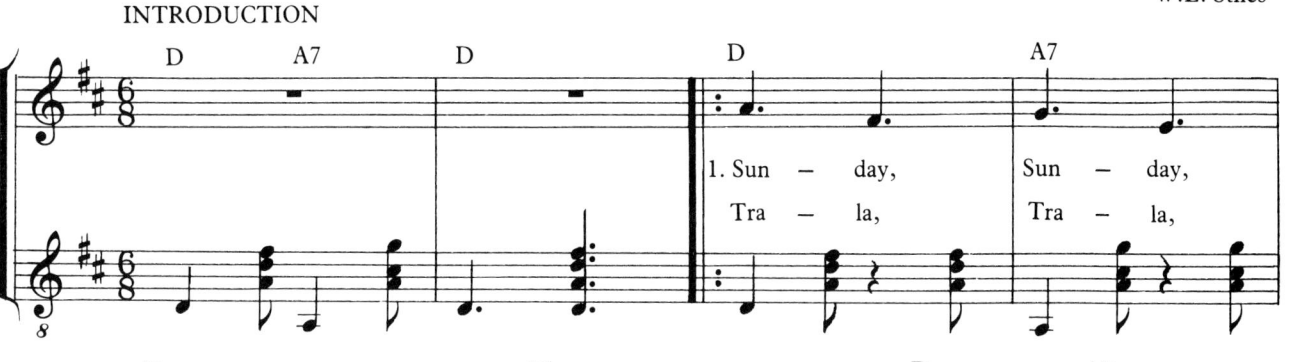

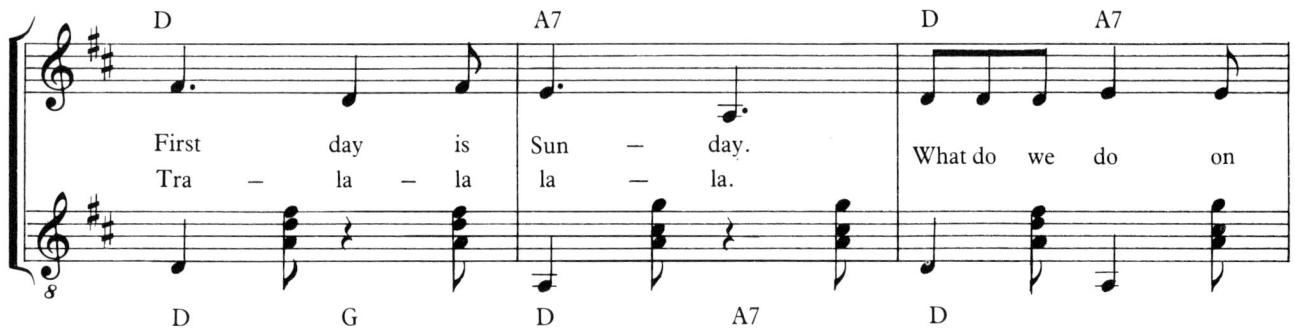

1. Sun — day, Sun — day,
   First day is Sun — day.
   What do we do on Sun — day? We walk, walk, walk.

   Tra — la, Tra — la,
   Tra — la la la — la.

2. Monday, Monday,
   Second day is Monday.
   What do we do on Monday?
   We walk, walk, walk.
   Tra-la tra-la,
   Tra-la-la-la-la.
   What do we do on Monday?
   We walk, walk, walk.

3. Tuesday – slide 
4. Wednesday – run
5. Thursday – tip tip toe
6. Friday – jump 
7. Saturday – hop

The entire group may do this together. Stand still at first until the question is asked. When the 'Tra-la's' start perform the actions.

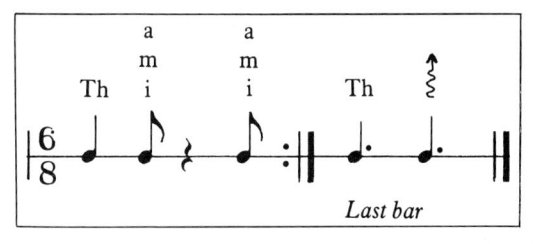

Last bar

I am a sundial, and I make a botch of
what is done far better by a watch. 

OR

I am a sundial, and I make a botch of
what is done far better by a watch. 

Hillaire Belloc

A Valentine song

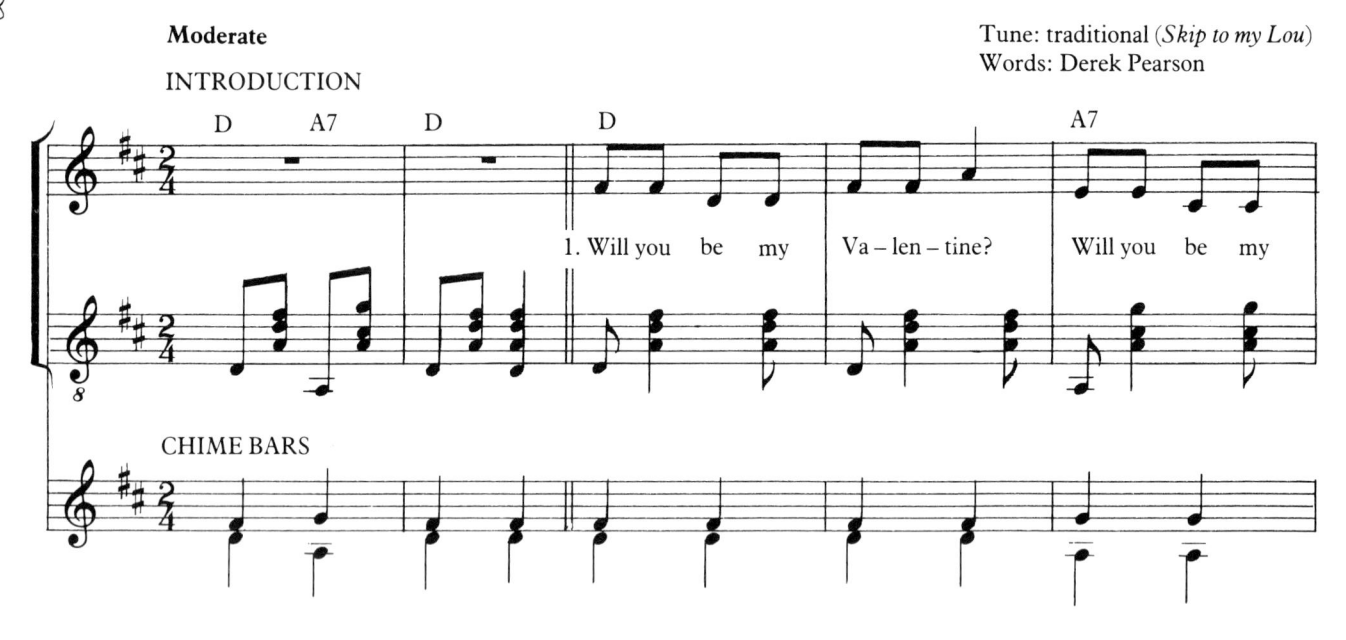

Moderate

INTRODUCTION

Tune: traditional (*Skip to my Lou*)
Words: Derek Pearson

CHIME BARS: A D F# G

1. Will you be my Valentine? Will you be my Valentine? Will you be my Valentine? I love you, my darling.

2 Yes, I'll be your Valentine . . .
   I love you, my darling.

3 I give you my card today . . .
   I love you, my darling.

4 Thank you for your card today . . .
   I love you, my darling

Add other verses as desired, Verses 3 and 4 can be repeated for the exchange of cards.

Children could make their own cards by cutting out a heart-shape in red paper and pasting it on to the front of a piece of folded thin card. This could be decorated and a message written inside. The heart-shape could be drawn (or traced) on to the paper and then coloured or painted if 'cutting out' is not possible.

Additional verses

Time verses

Can you tell what time it is . . . ?
Look the clock can tell you.

Short hand tells you all the hours . . .
Which one is it saying?

Long hand tells you minutes now . . .
Can you say how many?

Both together tell the time . . .
What time is it now, please?

Zoo verses

We are going to visit the zoo . . .
Wonder what we'll see there?

Elephant and polar bear,
Tall giraffe just standing there,

Llama with his nose in the air,
At the zoo this morning.

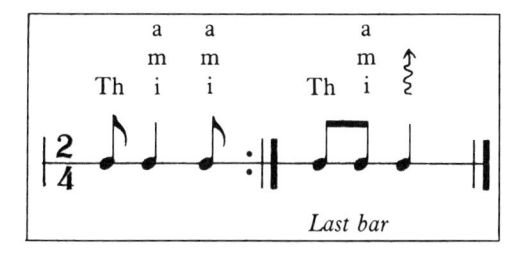

Add other verses for other animals and other events.

1 Easter bunnies hop around . . .
   Hop and hop and hop and stop.
2 Holidays are here again . . .
   Have a lovely holiday.
3 Something very special today . . .
   This is Michael's birthday.*
4 Running, running all around . . .
   When you hear the drum — STOP.*
5 Now lie down and have a sleep (rest) . . .
   Everyone is quiet now.
6 Look there's lots and lots of snow . . .
   Build a snowman big and round.
7 Squeeze the snowball till it's round . . .
   Knock the snowman's hat off.
8 Fireworks bang and rockets woosh . . .
   Stand well back for safety.
9 Turnip lanterns bright and round . . .
   Hallowe'en is here now.
10 Ghosts are floating round the sky,
   Witches on their broomsticks fly,
   Round and round and round the sky
   Hallowe'en is here now.

Make ghosts and witches, as fantastic as possible, and hang them up with fine black thread to give the impression of flying.

* V.3 Substitute the various children's names here, adjusting rhythm to fit.
* V.4 Also walking, hopping, etc. here.
  V.5 Sing this verse slowly and quietly.
  V.7 Mime the actions here.
  V.9 Can you name other objects with similar shape? Make a list and count them.

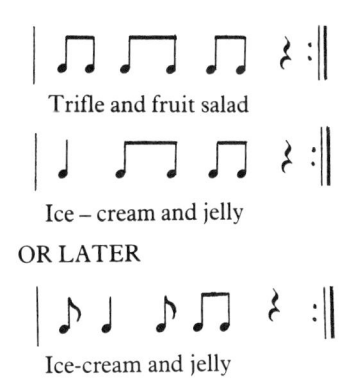

A birthday party

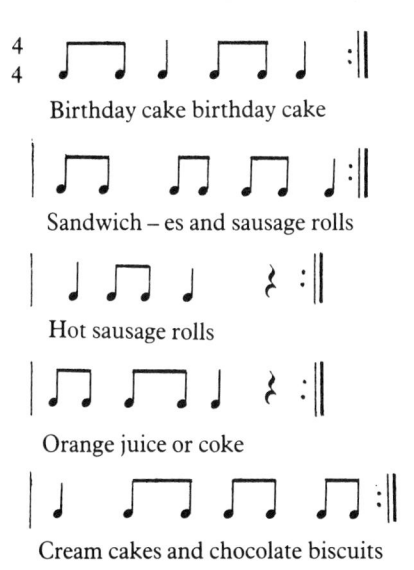

Birthday cake birthday cake

Sandwich – es and sausage rolls

Hot sausage rolls

Orange juice or coke

Cream cakes and chocolate biscuits

Trifle and fruit salad

Ice – cream and jelly

OR LATER

Ice-cream and jelly

Use the various phrases and rhythms individually at first, then put together as many as the children can manage. It will probably help to keep things steady if they mark the pulse by clapping quietly (two fingers on the palm of the other hand) or tapping gently on a desk or table. Add any other phrases and rhythms you like, especially those the children invent themselves.

Happy birthday

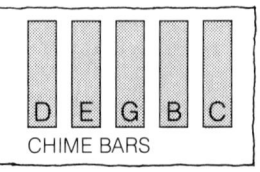

Steady, do not hurry

Words and music (Part one): Derek Pearson
(Part two): Mildred and Patty Hill

Please tell me do, How old are you? How old are you to-day? I'm ... years old to-day. ...1 2 3 4 5 6 7 etc.

In 'Happy Birthday' (last eight bars) the words can be changed to:

Happy Christmas to you (*shake hands with your neighbours*)
Happy Christmas to you
Happy Christmas dear everyone (*or somebody's name here*)
Happy Christmas to you.

or 'Happy Easter to you'.

There are many other possibilities for this type of greeting:

Thank you Mum for my tea, etc.
Thank you John for your help, etc.
Thank you God for the rain, (sun, flowers, etc.)
Thank you all very much, etc.

The whole group join in singing the first section. Then the person whose birthday it is plays the number of years on the 'G' chime bar with the class joining in counting. Then everyone sings 'Happy Birthday to you' in the last section.

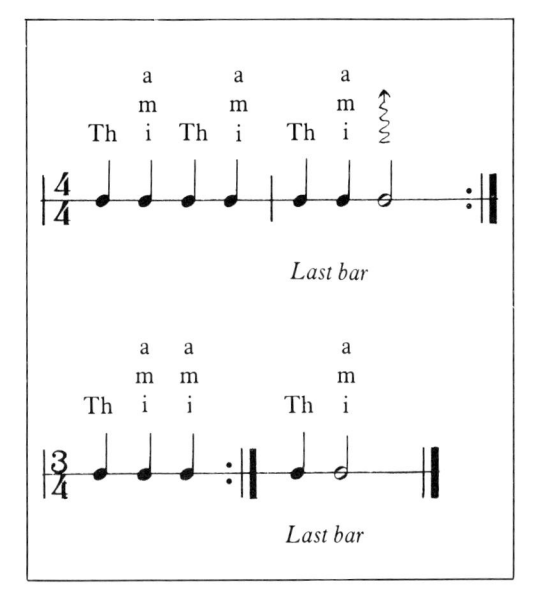

The seasons

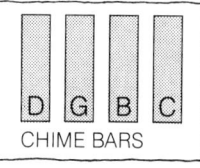

Moderate

INTRODUCTION

Tune: traditional German
Words (v.1): trans. Derek Pearson
(v.2–5): Derek Pearson

CHIME BARS: D G B C

CHIME BARS

ALTERNATIVE SIMPLE CHIME BAR PART

Lyrics:

1. Now there are four sea-sons that make up the year. I'll tell you how I know which sea-son is here.

2. In winter it's cold, oh there's ice and there's snow,
   And nobody likes it, we wish it would go.

3. The spring brings the buds and the leaves and the flowers,
   Now every day seems to be longer by hours.

4. The summer has birds singing loud in the trees,
   We lie in the sunshine, and buzz go the bees.

5. In autumn the harvest is gathered in store,
   The farmer has started his ploughing once more.

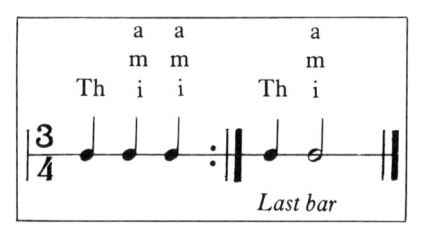

Chime bar part Pattern A: play once for the Introduction and twice for each verse.

Spring

The brushes and pans come out.
The housewife begins to shout,
  'You take the duster
  You take the pan
  You take the brush
And make everything spick and span.'

The forks and spades come out.
The gardener begins to shout,
  'You take the fork,
  You take the spade,
  You fetch the water,
Or the flowers will start to fade.'

The tractors and the ploughs come out.
The farmer begins to shout,
  'You take the tractor,
  You take the plough,
  You take the sower,
And do it right now!'

Heather West

Thaw

Over the land freckled with snow half-thawed
The speculating rooks at their nests cawed
And saw from the elm-tops, delicate as flowers of grass,
What we below could not see, Winter pass.

Edward Thomas

The green spring

When spring comes
I see the woods turning green,
The water in the river turning green,
The hills turning green,
The fields turning green,
The little beetles turning green,
And even the white-bearded old man turning green,
The green blood
Nurtures the fatigued earth,
And from the earth bursts forth
A green hope.

Shan Mei

The grasshopper

A young grasshopper
Whose name was Fred,
Was told by his mother
To go to bed.
But the night was hot,
He couldn't sleep,
So out of the window, with a leap
To jump about and stretch his knees
Till catching cold, he gave a sneeze.
Leaping back he banged his nut,
His sneeze had blown the window shut!

Jeremy Lloyd

Timesquare

M	I	N	U	T	E
D	A	Y	S	O	V
A	W	E	E	K	E
Y	E	A	R	A	N
E	A	R	L	Y	P
H	O	U	R	A	M

Copy on to an O.H.P transparency with a permanent black pen. Then as the children find each word outline it in a bright colour with a water-washable pen. When finished with the transparency wipe off the coloured lines with a damp cloth or tissue for use again later.

  The words are all from left to right, or top to bottom. The children should know this when they start. Make up simpler, or more complicated versions to suit the children you are working with.

April Fool

Not too fast
Author unknown

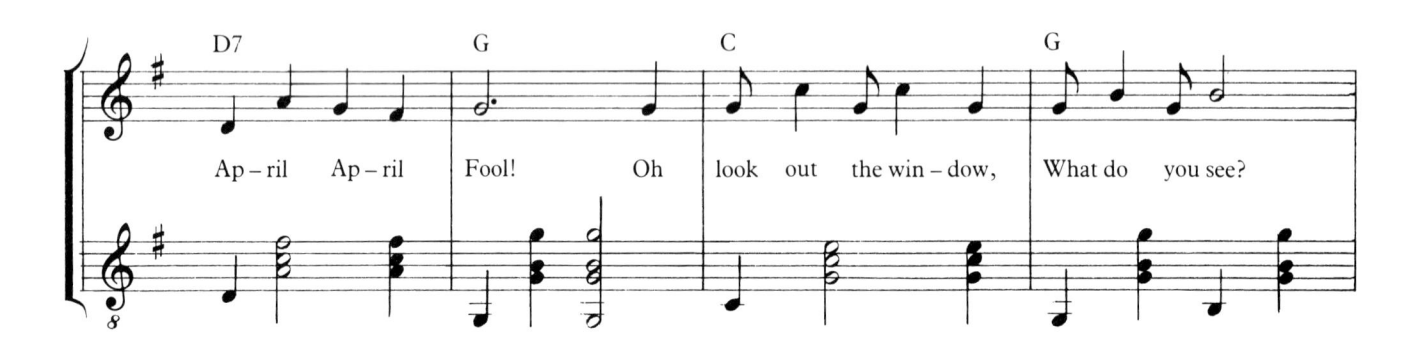

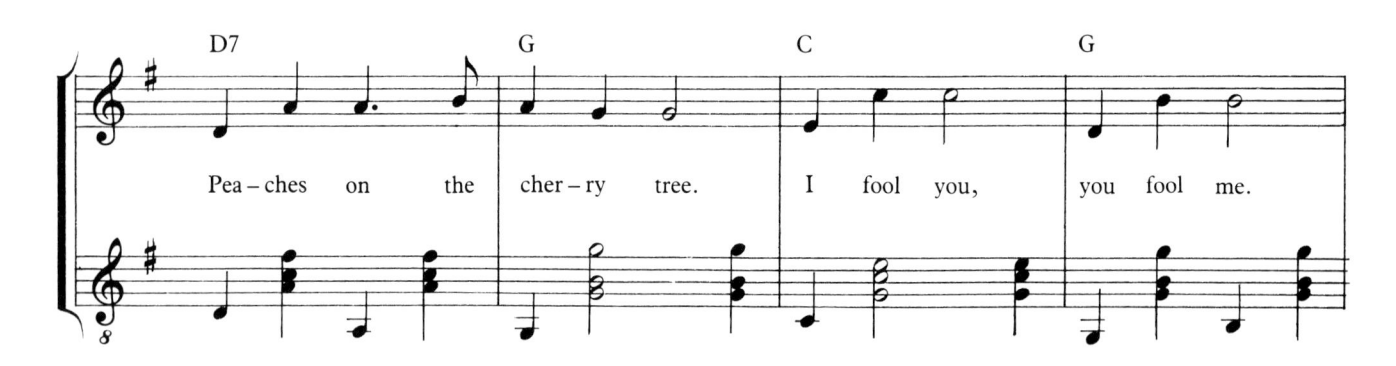

INTRODUCTION VERSES 1–3

1. Your hair is the co-lour of to-ma-to soup,
Ap-ril Fool, Ap-ril Fool! There's a great big go-ril-la in the chi-cken coop,
Ap-ril Ap-ril Fool! Oh look out the win-dow, What do you see?
Pea-ches on the cher-ry tree. I fool you, you fool me.

58

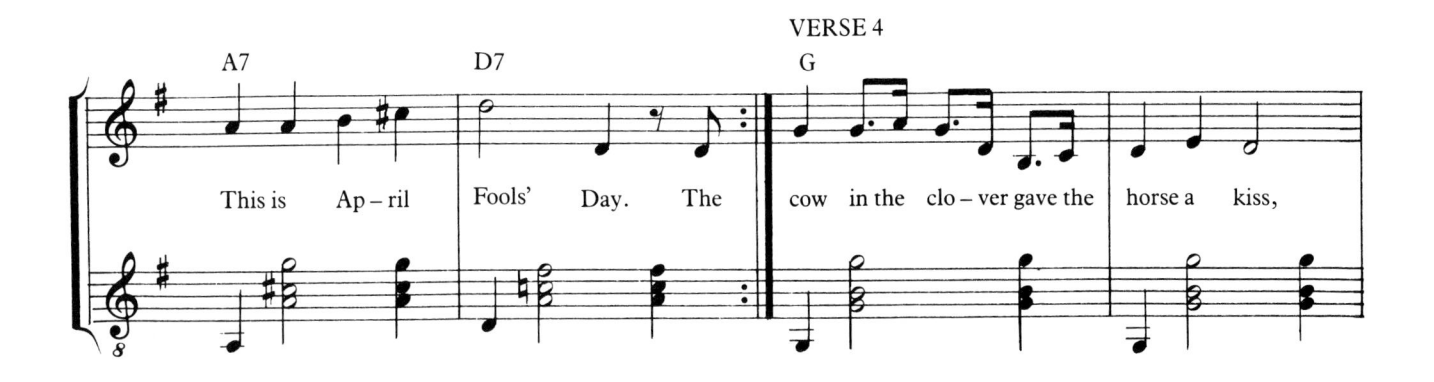

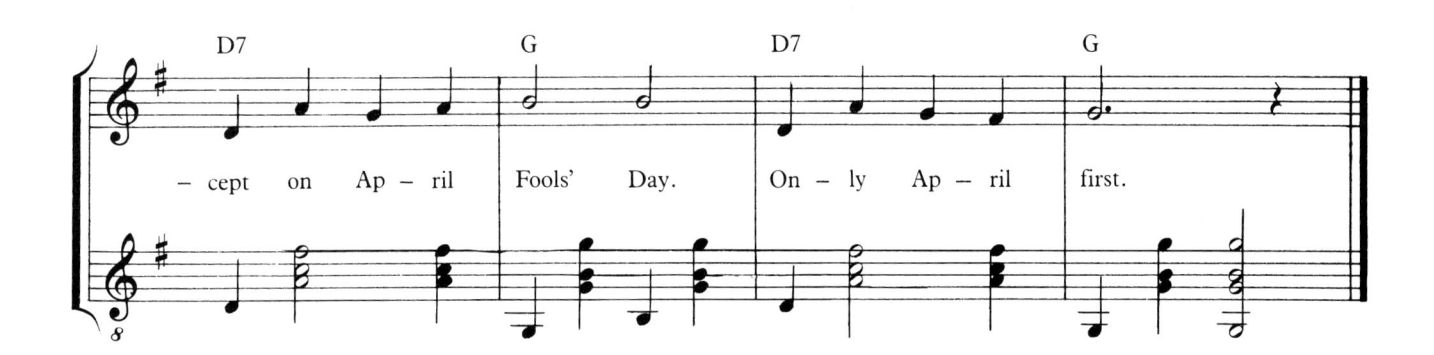

2. The cat's in the middle of the custard pie, April Fool, April Fool!
   There's a dog in the kitchen and he's ten feet high, April April Fool!
   Oh look out the window . . .

3. The pig in the parlour has a big cigar, April Fool, April Fool!
   There's a two headed elephant in daddy's car, April April Fool!
   Oh look out the window . . .

4. (*as written*)

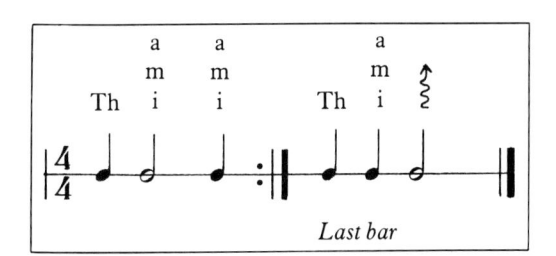

Everybody loves Saturday night

Traditional

Not too fast, bouncy rhythm

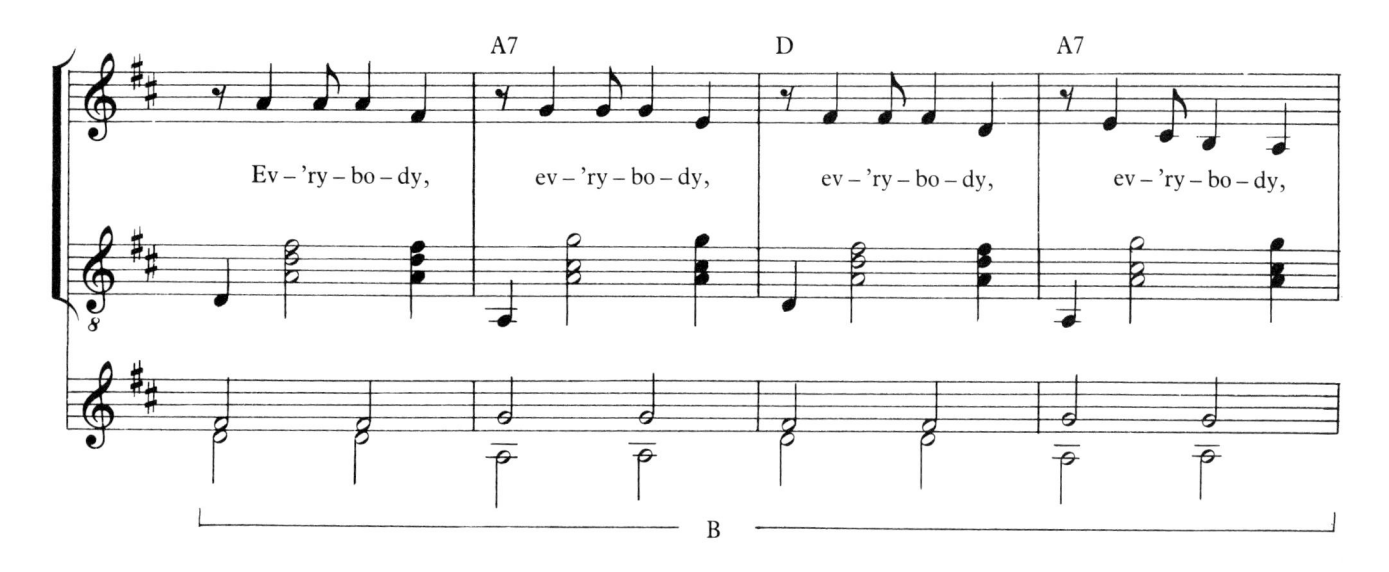

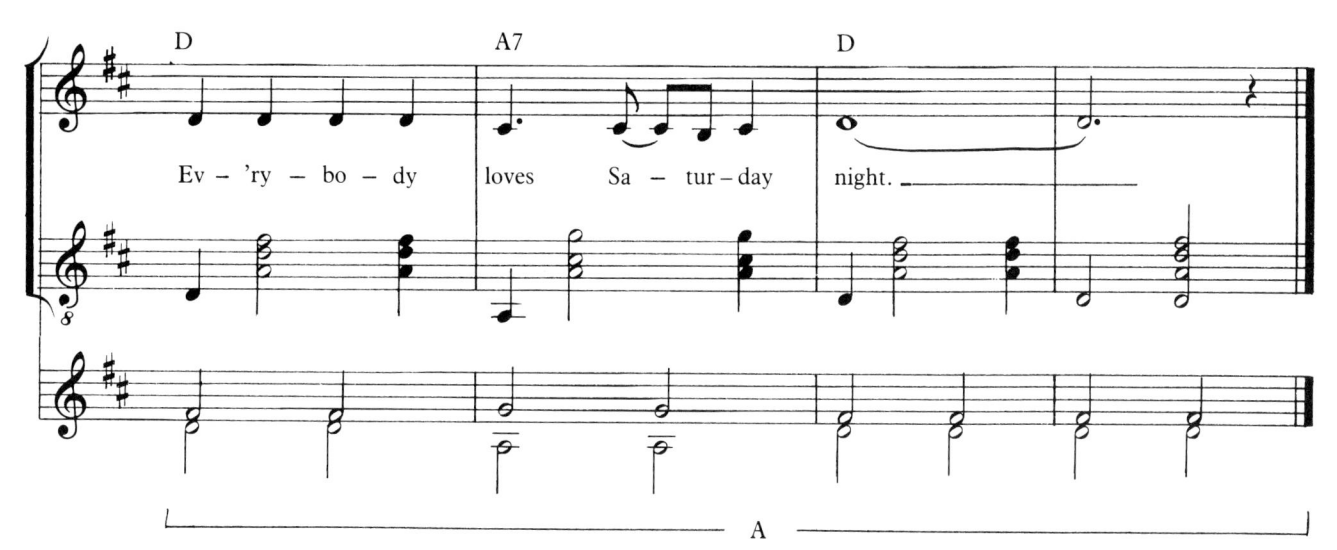

Additional verses

1. Everybody loves coming to school! etc.
2. Everybody loves/hates Monday morning/at nine.
3. Everybody loves Friday at four.
4. Everybody loves going to swim.
5. Everybody loves having a dance (*Three times*)
   It's a disco (*Four times*)
   Everybody loves having a dance.

Modify or adjust to suit the needs of the children involved. Add other verses to suit your own situation.

The auto-harp would play the guitar chords as indicated.

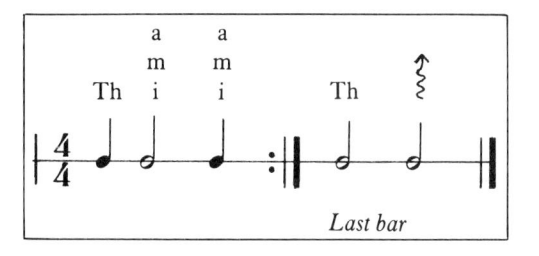

The chime bar part breaks down into two patterns, **A** and **B**. **A** is played once for the Introduction and three times for the verse. **B** is itself two two-bar patterns and is played after the second **A** pattern in the verse, then **A** returns to finish, i.e. $\frac{\text{Intro}}{\text{A}} \frac{\text{Verse}}{\text{A A B A}}$. Teach pattern **A** and sing the song with chime bars silent where pattern **B** enters. When this is secure teach pattern **B** and fit into place. It is good to start with two groups, one playing **A** and the other playing **B**.

Pray God bless/ Round the seasons

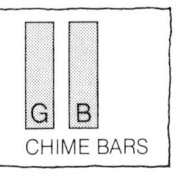

Very steady, not fast

INTRODUCTION

Tune: Traditional English
Words (*Round the seasons*): Derek Pearson

CHIME BARS

Lyrics: Pray God bless All friends here, A very merry Christmas And a happy New Year.

2. Spring is here,
   Bright and clear.
   It's March and April also May,
   Yes, spring is here.

3. Summer's come
   Sun and fun,
   June, July and August
   All make summer and sun.

4. Autumn now,
   Gather logs.
   September and October
   With November all fogs.

5. Winter's sneeze,
   Cough and wheeze.
   December, January, February,
   Yes, it's winter's long freeze.

The chime bar part can be extended to include all available G, B and D notes. Keep G the lowest and the most prominent in sound. The part can be reduced to just a single note G played by one person or expanded to include as many as notes are available.

Descant recorders can play the melody. It could start as a 2-part round, with children entering at 1 and 3. Then when they are really confident bring them in at 2 and 4.

As a Christmas carol or round this could have other words added to those given. When used as a seasons' round it is probably best to sing it first as a unison song, and then use as a round. As a 'round-up' of the year the four verses could be sung as a unison song if desired.

December music

As I went into the city, clattering chimes
Carolled December music over the traffic
And I remembered my childhood, the times
Of deep snow, the same songs.

Cars meshed in the rain, horns snarled, brakes
Cursed against trolleys, and the neon evening
Blurred past my cold spectacles, the flakes
Of the iron songs scattered.

I stood near a corner drugstore trying to hear,
While all the weather broke to pouring water,
The drowned phrases between those coming clear
Though of course I knew all.

The notes my mind sang over would not do
To knit the shattered song as I wanted it,
Wanted it bell to bell as it once rang through
To its triumphant end.

It was no matter what I had left to believe
On a flooded pavement under a battering sign,
Clutching my hat while rain ran in my sleeve
And my bifocals fogged.

It was only to think of my childhood, the deep snow,
The same songs, and Christmas Eve in the air,
And at home everyone in the world I knew
All together there.

Winifred Townley Scott

The pines

Hear the rumble,
Oh, hear the crash.
The great trees tumble.
The strong boughs smash.

Men with saws
Are cutting the pines –
That marched like soldiers
In straight green lines.

Seventy years
Have made them tall.
It takes ten minutes
To make them fall.

And breaking free
With never a care,
The pine cones leap
Through the clear, bright air.

M. Mahy

Death of a snowman

I was awake all night,
Big as a polar bear,
Strong and firm and white.
The tall black hat I wear
Was draped with ermine fur.
I felt so fit and well
Till the world began to stir
And the morning sun swell.
I was tired, began to yawn;
At noon in the humming sun
I caught a severe warm;
My nose began to run.
My hat grew black and fell,
Was followed by my grey head.
There was no funeral bell,
But by tea-time I was dead.

Vernon Scannell

Christmas dinner

1 Soup or fruit juice

2 Hot roast turkey

3 Sausa – ges and stuffing

4 Sprouts and roast po – tatoes

5 Christmas pud or mince pies

OR

6 Christmas pudding or mince pies

Mark the pulse by gently clapping, or quietly tapping on a tambour, at first to keep it steady. Watch the rhythm on 'soup or fruit juice'. If the rests at the end of 2 and 3 prove tricky, add in 'Yum' at the end of each in place of the rest. This should help to steady it. Add other phrases and rhythms to suit the children.

The weather

What's the weather on about?
Why is the rain so down on us?
Why does the sun glare at us so?

Why does the hail dance so prettily?
Why is the snow such an overall?
Why is the wind such a tearaway?

Why is the mud so fond of our feet?
Why is the ice so keen to upset us?
Who does the weather think it is?

Gavin Ewart

The twelve months

Snowy, Flowy, Blowy,
Showery, Flowery, Bowery,
Hoppy, Croppy, Droppy,
Breezy, Sneezy, Freezy.

George Ellis

Autumn's passing

Bonfire smoke swirls upward
Golden leaves fall down
Nuts and berries show themselves
Red and shining brown.

Swallows now have left us
Flown across the seas
Squirrels are so busy
Storing nuts in trees.

Hedgehog is bed-making
Ready for his sleep
Robin, gay and curious
Stops to take a peep.

Listen to the rustle
Where crisp leaves are found
Strewn in many colours
Carpeting the ground.

Who then can be passing
This bright wind-swept day?
Surely it is Autumn
Going on her way.

Hilda I. Rostrom

Glass falling

The glass is going down. The sun
Is going down. The forecasts say
It will be warm, with frequent showers.
We ramble down the showery hours
And amble up and down the day.
Mary will wear her black goloshes
And splash the puddles on the town;
And soon on fleets of mackintoshes
The rain is coming down, the frown
Is coming down of heaven showing
A wet night coming, the glass is going
Down, the sun is going down.

Louis MacNeice

Bonfire night

Watch the fireworks whizzing round,
Round and round along the ground.
Up they go into the sky
High, high, so very high.

Watching the jumping jack go round,
Round and round along the ground.
Watch the rocket going up,
Mounting skyward, up and up.

Take a sparkler, watch it spark,
Sparkling brightly in the dark.
Watch the fire so burning bright,
Blazing warmly in the night.

R. Brighton

Snow storm

What a night! The wind howls, hisses, and but stays
To howl more loud, while the snow volley keeps
Incessant batter at the window pane.
Making out comfort feel as sweet again;
And in the morning, when the tempest drops,
At every cottage door mountainous heaps
Of snow lie drifted, that all entrance stops
Until the besom and the shovel gain
The path, and leave a wall on either side.

John Clare

A name carol

At an easy lilting pace

Moravian carol

INTRODUCTION

Jo-na-than, Bar-ba-ra, Ti-mo-thy and Ma-ry, Hur-ry on to Beth-le-hem to the low-ly stab-le. Come and see the Ba-by small, Sleep-ing in the cat-tle stall. Hur-ry now on your way, To our Sa-viour born to-day.

The Introduction can be played twice if preferred. Use also between verses. Add other verses by using the names of children in the class. Some minor rhythm changes would occasionally be necessary and quite acceptable. If the low A in the second last bar is found to be awkward, sing the same note (A) as on the word 'born' at the start of the bar. If this A is used the descant recorder could play the melody.

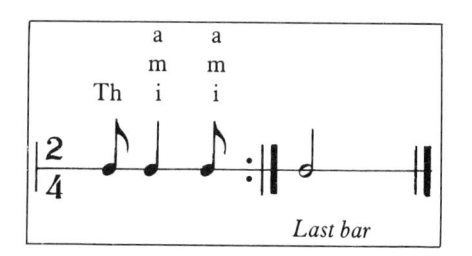

The donkey's Christmas

Plodding on,
From inn to inn,
No room to spare,
No room but a stable bare.
We rest,
And the following morning Jesus is born.
I gaze on the wondrous sight.
The King is born,
The King in a stable.
I see great lights,
Lights that are angels,
Everyone comes to see this sight.
I carried Mary,
Holy Mary,
Last night.

Stars, songs, faces

Gather the stars if you wish it so.
Gather the songs and keep them.
Gather the faces of women.
Gather the keeping years and years.
And then . . .
Loosen you hands, let go and say good-bye
    Let the stars and songs go.
    Let the faces and years go.
    Loosen your hands and say good-bye.

Carl Sandburg

O men from the fields

O men from the fields!
Come gently within.
Tread softly, softly,
O men coming in!
Mavourneen is going
From me and from you,
Where Mary will fold him
With mantle of blue!

From reek of the smoke,
And cold of the floor,
And the peering of things
Across the half-door.
O men from the fields!
Soft, softly come through –
Mary puts round him
Her mantle of blue.

Padraic Colum

The witnesses

The Innkeeper's wife:
It was a night in winter.
Our house was full, tight-packed as salted herrings –
So full, they said, we had to hold our breaths
To close the door and shut the night air out!
And then two travellers came. They stood outside
Across the threshold, half in the ring of light
And half beyond it. I would have let them in
Despite the crowding – the woman was past her time –
But I'd no mind to argue with my husband,
The flagon in my hand and half the inn
Still clamouring for wine. But when the trade slackened,
And all our guests had sung themselves to bed
Or told the floor their troubles, I came out here
Where he had lodged them. The man was standing
As you are now, his hand smoothing that board.
He was a carpenter, I heard them say.
She rested on the straw, and on her arm
A child was lying. None of your creased-faced brats
Squalling their lungs out. Just lying there
As calm as a new-dropped calf – his eyes wide open,
And gazing around as if the world he saw
In the chaff-strewn light of the stable lantern
Was something beautiful and new and strange.

Clive Sansom

Christmas

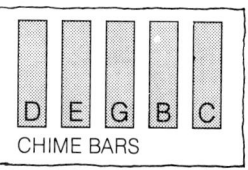

Slowly and steadily

Russian carol

CHIME BARS: D E G B C

INTRODUCTION

1. Stars are shin-ing bright-ly,
Bells ring-ing loud-ly, Glo-ri-a.

2 Shepherds sleeping were woken by An-gels singing Glori-a.

3 King's from far with gifts so precious and rare, sing Glori-a.

4 Sing all people on earth for peace and good will, Glori-a.

Verse 2 could start quietly and gradually get louder. Add other verses about seasons or festivals as required. The melody could be played on a descant recorder.

Hear the glad tidings

Mazurka time, happily

Polish carol
Words: trans. Ruth Heller

INTRODUCTION

1. Hear the glad ti-dings, hear the glad ti-dings! Now in Beth-lehem man-ger. Born of the Vir-gin, born of the Vir-gin is the Christ, our Sa-viour.

CHORUS

An-gels are sing-ing, kings gifts are bring-ing, Shep-herds are pray-ing, cat-tle are kneel-ing To the lit-tle Je-sus, to the son of Ma – ry, He is born to us this day.

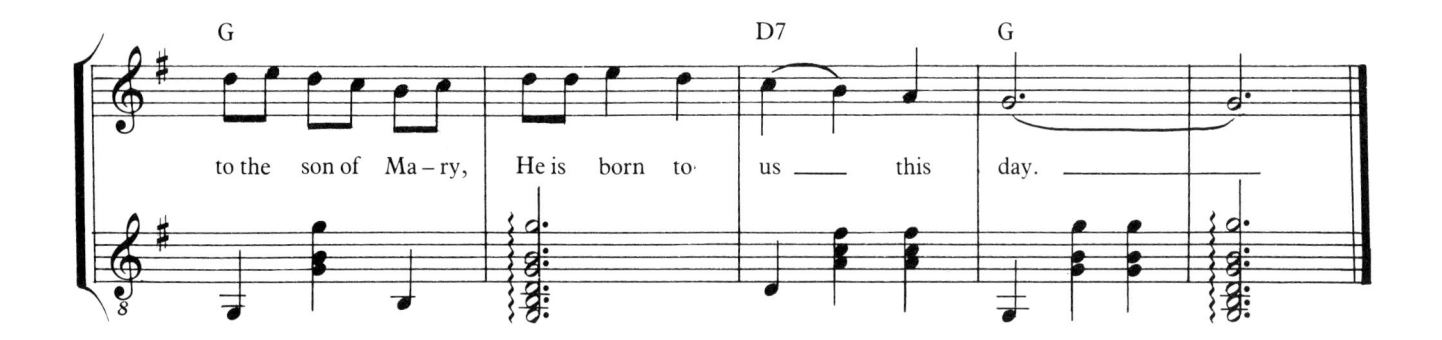

2. No room for Mary, no room for Mary,
   Full the inn with travellers.
   So to a stable, so to a stable
   Did she go for shelter.
   Angels are singing . . .

3. While Joseph watches, while Joseph watches,
   Safely Christ is sleeping.
   See Mary smiling, see Mary smiling
   As she rocks the king.
   Angels are singing . . .

4. Kneel we before him, kneel we before him,
   Hear our glad song ringing:
   'Glory to Jesus, Glory to Jesus,
   Glory everlasting!'
   Angels are singing . . .

The melody could be played on descant recorders.

New Year's wish

'I wish you as much luck and gain
As there are droplets in the rain,
Of blessings such a big supply
As there are starlets in the sky,
Of pleasures now so many more
Than there are sand grains on a shore –
And hope that all comes true!

'Thanks!' And the same to YOU!

Unknown

The prayer of the donkey

O God, who made me
to trudge along the road
always,
to carry heavy loads
always,
and to be beaten
always!
Give me great courage and
   gentleness.

One day let somebody understand me –
that I may no longer want to weep
because I can never say what I mean
and they make fun of me.
Let me find a juicy thistle –
and make them give me time to pick it.
And, Lord, one day, let me find again
my little brother of the Christmas crib.

Carmen B. de Gastold

Nature carol

Slowly and gently

Tune: traditional Filipino
Words: Malcolm Sargent

INTRODUCTION

1. Co-ral, am-ber, pearl and shell, Gifts we ga-ther from sum-mer seas. Find and bind, make love the spell. Take our gifts if they charm and please.

CHORUS

A-lo-ha! A-lo-ha! Ha-naw, ha-naw, a-lo-ha! A-lo-ha! A-lo-ha! Ha-naw, ha-naw, a-lo-ha!

Vs. 1–3 | Last time
— ha!

70

2 Ruby, onyx, rain and dew
   Weave a crown with your jewelled light.
   Show and know whose world is new,
   Who is prince of the day and night.
   Aloha! Aloha . . .

3 Meadow, orchard, field and wine 
   Melon, grape and maize are here,
   Leaf and sheaf with tendrils twine,
   Bring your harvests from far and near.
   Aloha! Aloha . . .

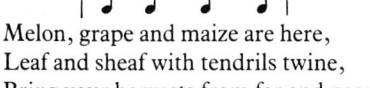

4 Mountains, flowers, trees and hills
   Laugh and sing where his blessing fall,
   Wind and waves, lagoons and rills
   Shout his love who is Lord of all.
   Aloha! Aloha . . .

This is not really a Christmas carol, but can very readily be sung then. It makes a very pleasant addition to the usual Christmas repertoire, but can be sung at other times equally well.

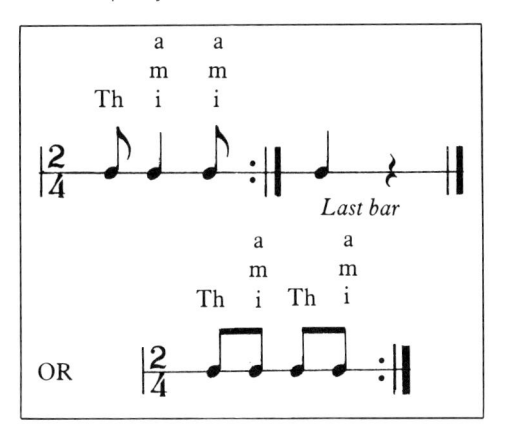

Adieu

I left the little birds
And the sweet lowing of the herds,
And couldn't find out words,
   Do you see,
To say to them good-bye,
Where the yellowcups do lie;
So heaving a deep sigh,
   Took to sea . . .

John Clare

The autumn robin

Sweet little bird in russet coat
The livery of the closing year,
I love thy lonely plaintive note
And tiny whispering song to hear
While on the stile or garden seat
I sit to watch the falling leaves,
The song thy little joys repeat
My loneliness relieves.

John Clare

in just

in just –
spring when the world is mud -
luscious the little
lame balloonman

whistles far and wee
and eddieandbill come
running from marbles and
piracies and it's
spring

when the world is puddle-wonderful

the queer
old balloonman whistles
far and wee
and bettyandisobel come dancing
from hop-scotch and jump-rope and

it's
spring
and
  the
     goatfooted

balloonman whistles
far
and
wee

e. e. cummings

THE WORLD ABOUT US

Disadvantaged children need to find out about their environment. Their experience is often very limited. All children have to realize themselves as people and find a place in society relating to those around them. In doing so they realize their dependence on others as well as the fact that they too have something to give. Everyone is inter-dependent — 'No man is an island'. Music can contribute to this development. Use the songs, poems, activities, games, and anything you can devise to enrich your children's understanding.

The cabbage patch	*73*
An alphabet song	*74*
Mail song	*75*
The postman	*77*
Colour song	*78*
Mary wore her red dress	*80*
The haunted house	*82*
Roses from Fyn	*86*
I went to visit a farm	*88*
Incy wincy spider	*90*
Tommy Thumb	*94*
Down by the station	*96*
Morningtown ride	*98*
A turkey ran away	*100*
Sing a rainbow	*102*

The cabbage patch

Language development
Rhyming words
Group participation

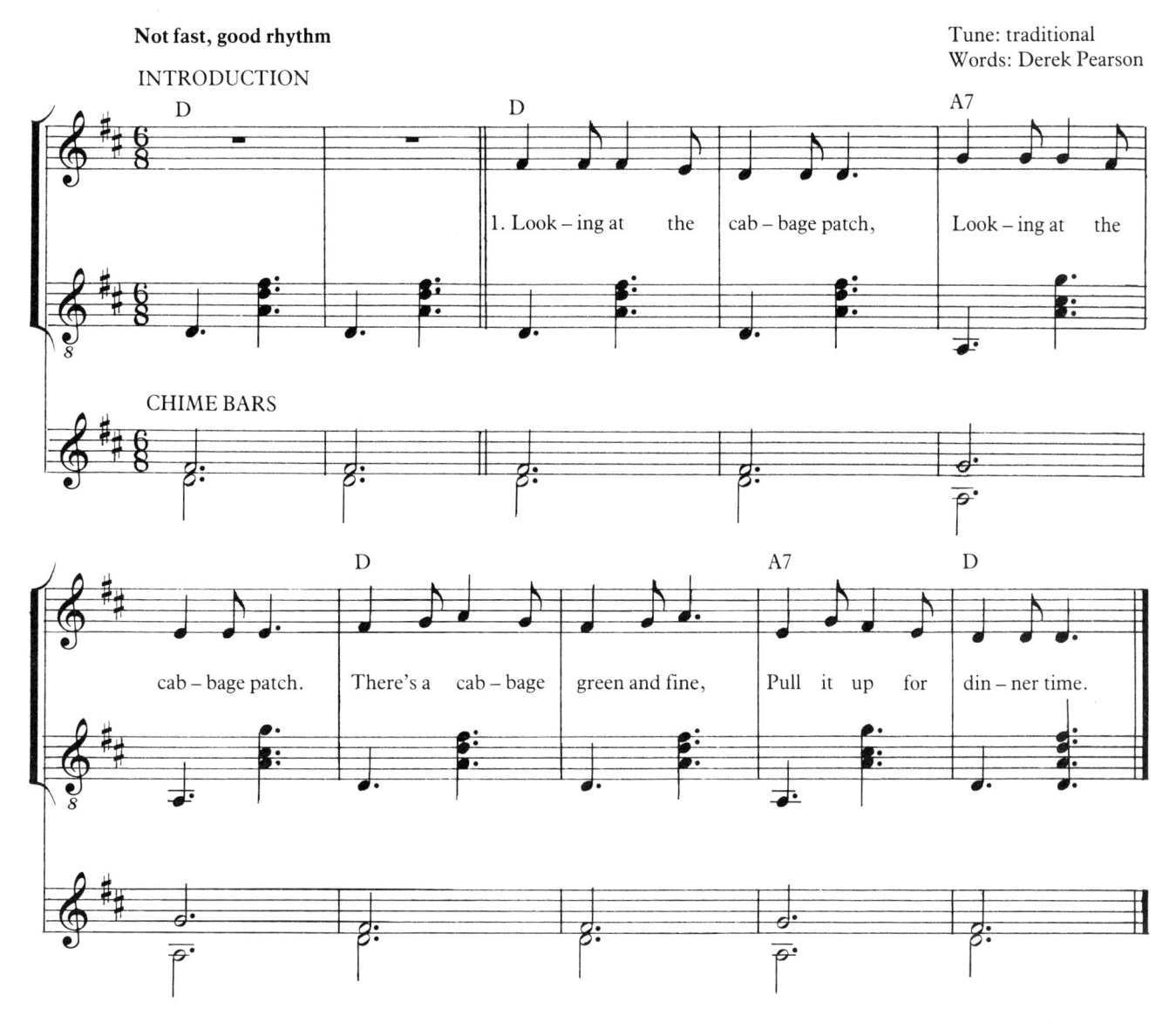

Not fast, good rhythm

INTRODUCTION

Tune: traditional
Words: Derek Pearson

1. Look – ing at the cab – bage patch, Look – ing at the cab – bage patch. There's a cab – bage green and fine, Pull it up for din – ner time.

CHIME BARS

2. Chop it up and cook it quick,
   Chop it up and cook it quick.
   Knob of butter, pinch of spice,
   Eat it up it tastes so nice.

3. Chop it fine and finer still,
   Chop it fine and finer still.
   Making coleslaw for our tea,
   Lots for you and lots for me.

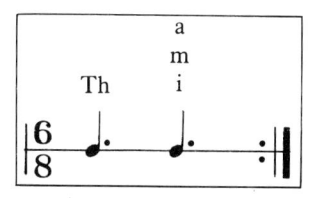

CHIME BARS: A D F# G

Invent actions to suit different activities. What is coleslaw? Could you make some? In verse 2 the 'spice' referred to is nutmeg. Just a pinch on cabbage is delicious.

Chime bars could play two chords in each bar if desired. The lower notes only of the chime bar part need to be played if a simple part is required. In this case play the 'D' with the R.H. and the 'A' with the L.H.

73

Oats and beans and barley grow

'Oats and beans and barley grow' uses the same tune as 'The cabbage patch'. (It is sometimes known as 'Oats and peas and barley grow', also 'Oats, peas, beans, and barley grow'. Take your pick!)

1. Oats and beans and barley grow (*Twice*)
   You or I or nobody knows,
   How oats and beans and barley grow.

2. Thus the farmer sows his seed (*Twice*)
   He stamps his feet and claps his hands,
   and turns around to view his land.

3. Waiting for a partner (*Twice*)
   Open the ring and take her in,
   and kiss her when you get her in.

Some people know other verses to this song. Invent you own verses as you feel inclined. Simple actions can be added to fit in with the suggestions in the verses.

Growing cress

Grow some cress in the classroom and, if possible, make it into cress sandwiches. Some might not like its rather sharp taste. The great thing about this is the speed with which it grows. If planted on a Friday by Monday something is really happening.

An alphabet song

Use the tune of 'Twinkle, twinkle little star'.

The same tune is used for 'Little Arabella Millar'. (See *This Little Puffin*.)

Cardboard box quiz

Take a very large empty cardboard box and collect a number of objects that make 'everyday' sounds, e.g. keys, light switch, cup and saucer, coins, old clock or watch to wind up, cutlery, etc. Put them into the box to hide them from the children. (Add any sounds you want and vary to allow the game to be played a number of times.)

Ask the children to listen to the sounds and identify them (most likely by telling you each time, as it is unlikely they will be able, at this stage, to write them down).

This can also be played with chime bars (or xylophone, glockenspiel, etc.) – one high and one low note (later on, also one in the middle). Especially useful for identifying high and low pitch, and for helping children with a suspected hearing impairment. Play notes in different groupings and ask children to say what you played. Start by identifying the notes e.g. High – play it, Low – play it. Then play different patterns of two or three notes, occasionally with repeats of the same pitch. Extend as they become secure.

Mail song

Language development
Action song

Moderate with good rhythm

Woody Guthrie
Words (verses 2 and 3): Derek Pearson

INTRODUCTION

1. I'm gon-na wrap my-self in pa-per,
I'm gon-na daub my-self with glue,
Stick some stamps on top of my head,
I'm gon-na mail my-self to you.

2 I'm going to put myself in a pillar box
Off in a van to the G.P.O.,
Parcels, letters, cards and me,
I'm going to mail myself to you.

3 Knock on the door! "Oh, it's the postman",
Unwrap the parcel, see it's me.
Fill me up with bacon eggs,
Now that I've mailed myself to you.

Some slight rhythm changes will be needed to fit some words in verses 2 and 3. The Introduction may be played twice if desired. The descant recorder could play the melody.

The postman

Language development
Visual awareness

Moderate speed

Tune: Lee Kjelson
Words (Verse 1): Lee Kjelson
(Verse 2): Derek Pearson

INTRODUCTION

1. The postman comes around ev'ry day, ev'ry day. The postman comes around ev'ry day. Bringing letters, packages, books and papers too. Notes and bills for Mum and Dad, cards for me and you. The postman comes around ev'ry day, ev'ry day. The postman comes around ev'ry day.

76

2 The milkman comes around every day, every day.
The milkman comes around every day.
Milk in bottles, cream in tubs, eggs in boxes too.
Some for breakfast, some for tea, some for me and you.
The milkman comes around every day, every day.
The milkman comes around every day.

The introduction may be played twice if desired.

The descant recorder could play the melody.
Make up more verses with the children.

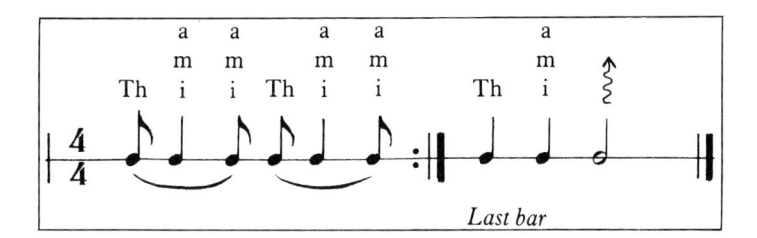

Night Mail

by W.H. Auden

The whole poem doesn't need to be used. Sections of it are marvellously rhythmical as well as being a source for further exploration of places, language, people and occupations.

Postman's knock

Rattat! Rattat!
There's the postman at the door,
He always knocks like that,
No matter who it's for,
It may be a letter,
And it may be a box,
O, I'm always very glad
When the postman knocks.

Rattat! Rattat!
Shall I run along to see,
If he is on the mat,
With something meant for me?
It may be just a postcard,
But it might be a box,
So I always run to look,
When the postman knocks.

Rodney Bennett

Watch the policeman

Watch the policeman in the street
Move his arms but not his feet;
   He only has to raise his hand,
   Cars and buses understand.
   He can make them stop and go,
   He can move them to and fro.
Watch the policeman in the street
Move his arms but not his feet.

Clive Sansom

Every Thursday morning
Before we're quite awake,
Without the slightest warning
The house begins to shake
With a Biff! Bang!
Biff! Bang! Biff!
It's the Dustman, who begins
Bang! Crash!
To empty all the bins
Of their rubbish and their ash
With a Biff! Bang! Biff! Bang! Bash!

Clive Sansom

Colour song

Visual awareness
Concentration

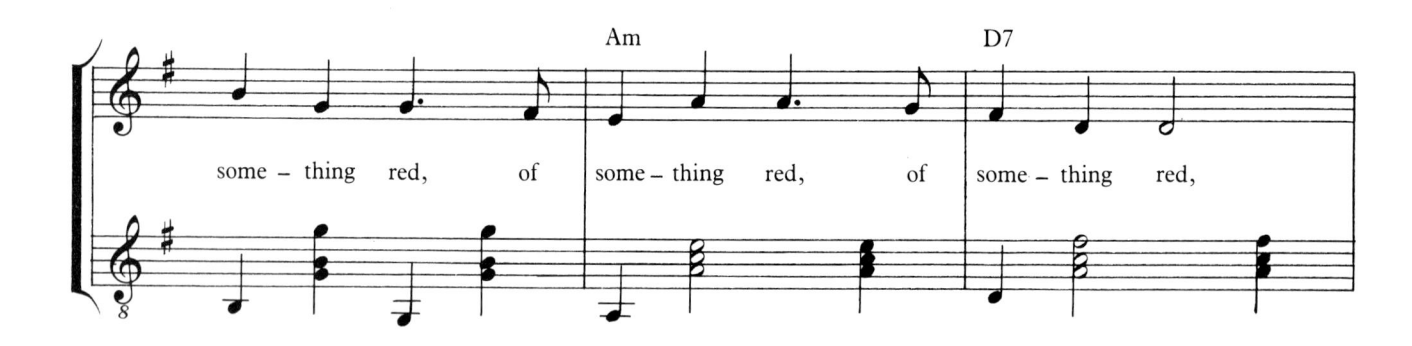

Steadily, not fast — Traditional

Red and yel-low, green and blue Red and yel-low, green and blue Red and yel-low, green and blue, Lis-ten to my song. Can you think of some-thing red? Yes, I can think of some-thing red, of some-thing red, of some-thing red,

Yes, I can think of some-thing red, Let's sing the song a - gain.

(See also *Sing a Rainbow*, pages 27 and 28)

After the first eight bars the teacher (later on one of the children) sings the question 'Can you think of something . . . ?' At first this may be something in the room, but later can move out into the wider environment, involving memory and imagination.

Accept their suggestions and discuss them together, then sing the second eight bars of the song. As suggested in the song, repeat with a different colour. It could also be sung to its original words, 'Do you know the Muffin man?'.

The descant recorder could play the melody.

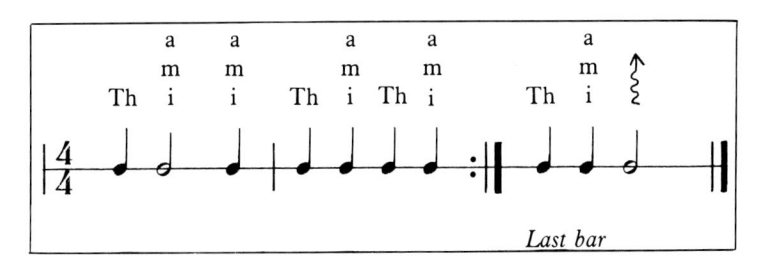

The paint box

'Cobalt and umber and ultramarine.
Ivory, black and emerald green –
What shall I paint to give pleasure to you?'
'Paint for me somebody utterly new.'

'I have painted you tigers in crimson and white.'
'The colours were good and you painted alright.'
'I have painted the cook and a camel in blue
And a panther in purple.' 'You painted them true.'

'Now mix me a colour that nobody knows,
And paint me a country where nobody goes,
And put in it people a little like you,
Watching a unicorn drinking the dew.'

E. V. Rieu

umber – earth brown

Isn't dressing depressing?

Isn't dressing depressing?
Button the buttons
Snap the snaps
Hook the hooks and
Zip the zippers
Tie the ties and
Strap the straps and
Clasp the clasps and
Slip the slippers
Buckle the buckles and
Knot the knots and
Pin the pins and
Lace the laces
Loop the loops and
Lock the locks and
Belt the belts and
Brace the braces –
What I like best is my own skin
That's the dress I'm always in.

Mary wore her red dress

Visual awareness
Language development
Group participation
Concentration

Quite steady

Traditional American children's song

INTRODUCTION

1. Mary wore her red dress, red dress, red dress, Mary wore her red dress all day long.

Additional verses could be:

2 Johnny wore his blue trousers.

3 Stephen wore his black shoes.

4 Jane wore her green coat.

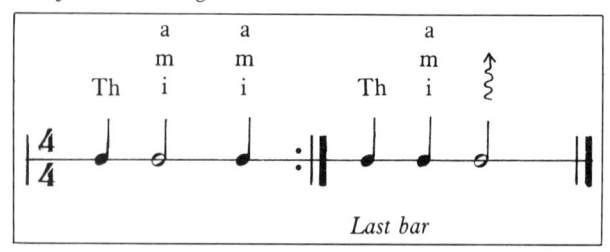

This can be adapted to any child, any colour, any garment, so its possibilities are almost endless. This tune is pentatonic (based on G).

CHIME BARS: D G B C

Here we go round the mulberry bush

This song, and many others has a multi-purpose facility that can exploit the old adage 'start from the known and move to the unknown'. Here are some verses to add to the original words:

This is the way we yawn and stretch . . .
When we get up in the morning.

This is the way we wash our face/hands/etc. . . .
When we get up in the morning.

This is the way we chop the wood . . .
To light the fire in the morning.

There are infinite other possibilities and similar lines, e.g.:

A Hallowe'en verse

Hallowe'en is here again,
The witches and hobgoblins cry.
Upon a broomstick, round the sky,
When midnight rings its warning.

Using a large suspended cymbal and soft beater, or a heavy triangle (with sides about 25 cm) make the 'clock' strike 12 midnight. Various dramatic actions could be devised for the end of the chimes, all based on the verse. A wall frieze could include witches on broomsticks, hobgoblins, a clock-tower, rooftops, a church-tower, the moon, clouds and trees in outline against the night sky. Parts of Robert Burns's poem *Tam O'Shanter* and Malcolm Arnold's overture of the same name would make interesting material. Use the Hallowe'en activity along with 'The haunted house' song if desired.

A band song

This is the way we play the drum, etc.
This is the way we play the drum, when we play in the band.

Last line
This is the way we play them all, etc.
This is the way we play them all, when we play in the band.

Play rhythm instruments on the beat and mime the other instruments. Put all together in the last verse. Involve *all* the children in playing, miming, etc.

'Here we go gathering nuts in May' uses the same tune.

Christmas verses

Here we go round the Christmas tree, the Christmas tree,
 the Christmas tree,
Here we go round the Christmas tree,
On Christmas day in the morning.

Presents round the Christmas tree, the Christmas tree,
 the Christmas tree,
Presents round the Christmas tree,
On Christmas day in the morning.

Yesterday

Yesterday
I had some thoughts
of Mummy
making me wear shorts
I know it's hot
but I will not!

The haunted house

Group participation
Action song
Creativity

Not fast, creepy
INTRODUCTION

Frère Jacques (minor key)
Words: Derek Pearson

Tip-toe, tip-toe, Tip-toe, tip-toe,
Up to the door, Up to the door. Oh, I do not like it,
Oh, I do not like it. Run, run, run. run, run, run!

CHIME BARS   2nd part (2 players)

simile for 7 bars to end

2 Tip toe, tip toe,
   Tip toe, tip toe,
   Knock on the door,
   Knock on the door,
   Here come big hobgoblins,
   Here come big hobgoblins,
   Run, run, run,
   Run, run, run.

3 Tip toe, tip toe,
   Tip toe, tip toe,
   Open the door
   Open the door,
   Look the house is empty,
   Look the house is empty,
   Ha ha ha,
   Ha ha ha.

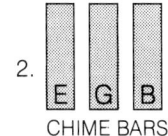

1. B E G CHIME BARS
2. E G B CHIME BARS

The second chime bar part requires two players for the chord but gives a fuller sound and is more effective. Add sounds for the 'Knock on the door' and the creaking of the door opening in verses 2 and 3 respectively. The tune is a minor key version of 'Frère Jacques'. If you want to do it in the major key, the guitar will play E major throughout. In the chime bar part, the note G will have to be G# throughout. I feel it is creepier in the minor key.

Additional verses

'The haunted house' is in E minor. To sing 'Frère Jacques' change the chord to E major for the guitar and the auto-harp. (See note above.)

1 Teacher: Where is Andrew? Where is Andrew?
             (other names)
   Child: Here I am, here I am.
   Teacher: How are you today?
   Child: I am very well.
   Class: Glad you're here, glad you're here.

2 Tip-toe, tip-toe,
   Tip-toe, tip-toe.
   Round the room, round the room,
   Running very quietly,
   Running very quietly,
   Now stand still, now stand still.

3 Jumping, jumping,
   Jumping, jumping,
   Up and down, up and down,
   Walking round and round,
   Walking round and round,
   Now all stop, now all stop.

Two's company

(The sad story of the man who didn't believe in ghosts)

They said the house was haunted, but
He laughed at them and said, 'Tut, tut!
I've never heard such tittle-tattle
As ghosts that groan and chains that rattle;
And just to prove I'm in the right,
Please leave me here to spend the night.'

They winked absurdly, tried to smother
Their ignorant laughter, nudged each other,
And left him just as dusk was falling
With a hunchback moon and screech-owls calling –
Not that this troubled him one bit;
In fact, he was quite glad of it,
Knowing it's every sane man's mission
To contradict all superstition.

But what is that? Outside it seemed
As if chains rattled, someone screamed!
Come, come, it's merely nerves, he's certain
(But just the same, he draws the curtain.)
The stroke of twelve – but there's no clock!
He shuts the door and turns the lock
(Of course, he knows that no one's there,
But no harm's done by taking care!)
Someone's outside – the silly joker,
(He may as well pick up the poker!)
That noise again! He checks the doors,
Shutters the windows, makes a pause
To seek the safest place to hide –
(The cupboard's strong – he creeps inside.)
'Not that there's anything to fear',
He tells himself, when at his ear
A voice breathes softly, 'How do you do!
I am a ghost. Pray, who are you?'

Raymond Wilson

hist whist

hist whist
little ghost things
tip-toe
twinkle-toe

little twitchy
witches and tingling
goblins
hob-a-nob hob-a-nob

little hoppy happy
toad in tweeds
tweeds
little itchy mousies

with scuttling
eyes rustle and run and
hidehidehide
whisk

whisk look out for the old woman
with the wart on her nose
what she'll do to yer
nobody knows

for she knows the devil oooh
the devil ouch
the devil
ach the great

green
dancing
devil
devil

devil
devil
      wheeEEEE

e. e. cummings

The horny-goloch

The horny-goloch is an awesome beast,
   Soople an' scaly;
It has two horns, an' a hantle o'feet,
   An' a forkie tailie.

The witch

Daughter of the moon, she rode by night,
Silhouetted in the sky, an eerie sight.
She sat on her broom with her painted hat,
Her black flowing robes, and of course, her cat.
Her wizened face was crabbed and old,
Her chin was sharp, with a wart I'm told.
Deep set and evil, those were her eyes,
And when she cast spells they doubled in size.
Her nose was hooked and had nostrils wide,
Her mouth was a slit, with large teeth inside.
Her fingers were thin, and bony, and strong.
Her nails were like talons and grotesquely long.
So beware, beware, for the moon is new,
Stay out of her path lest her curse falls on you.

K. Watts

The little witches

One little, two little, three little witches
Fly over haystacks, fly over ditches,
Slide down moonbeams without any britches –
Heigh ho, Hallowe'en's here!

Two witches

There was a witch
The witch had an itch,
The itch was so itchy it
Gave her a twitch.

Another witch
Admired the twitch
So she started twitching
Though she had no itch

Now both of them twitch
So it's hard to tell which
Witch has the itch and
Which witch has the twitch.

Alexander Resnikoff

This poem is a very good articulation exercise as well as being good fun.

The Hairy Toe

Once there was a woman went out to pick beans,
and she found a Hairy Toe.
She took the Hairy Toe home with her,
and that night, when she went to bed,
the wind began to moan and groan.
Away off in the distance
she seemed to hear a voice crying,
'Who's got my Hair-r-ry To-o-oe?
who's got my Hair-r-ry To-o-oe?'

The woman scrooched down,
way down under the covers,
and about that time
the wind appeared to hit the house,
Smoosh,
and the old house creaked and cracked
like something was trying to get in.
The voice had come nearer,
almost at the door now,
and it said,
'Where's my Hair-r-ry To-o-oe?
Who's got my Hair-r-ry To-o-oe?'

The woman scrooched further down
under the covers
and pulled them tight around her head.
The wind growled around the house
like some big animal
and r-r-um-mbled
over the chimbley.
All at once she heard the door cr-r-a-ack
and Something slipped in
and began to creep over the floor.
The floor went
cre-e-eak, cre-e-eak
at every step that thing took towards her bed.
The woman could almost feel
it bending over her bed,
Then in an awful voice it said:
'Where's my Hair-r-ry To-o-oe?
Who's got my Hair-r-ry To-o-oe?
You've got it!'

Great care must be taken when using poems or stories that might disturb some children to ensure that they understand it is purely fantasy and that when the dramatization of the poem is over everything is back to normal and nothing remains that might harm or upset them.

Sounds quiz

Take a cassette recorder with a 'built-in' microphone, or simple hand-operated microphone, and walk quietly round the house, school or wherever you decide to make up your quiz.

e.g. the 'Up and off to school' quiz:

> Alarm bell in morning
> Groan
> Footsteps
> Door opens – door closes
> Flush of toilet
> Water running – splashing
> Dressing sounds (Difficult to record. Possible to replace with music to cover dressing time.)
> Footsteps
> Rattle of cups and saucers, cutlery, etc.
> Time from radio
> 'Cheerio'. Door open – door close.

Then identify as many sounds as you can (write them down if possible). Again, a game of endless possibilities.

With many children you will need to play the tape twice, the first time right through, the second time stopping after each sound to let them identify and write down the sound, or tell someone. It may help you to identify each sound by a number so you can check easily. You could then call out the numbers before playing each sound.

If you go to a supermarket, railway station, etc., a small group of children could accompany you and see and hear the recordings being made. It doesn't really matter if occasionally one of their voices appears on the recording; it just adds reality.

Roses from Fyn

CHIME BARS: D G B C

Not fast, gently — Danish round

Chime bar pattern. Play four times.

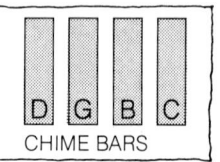

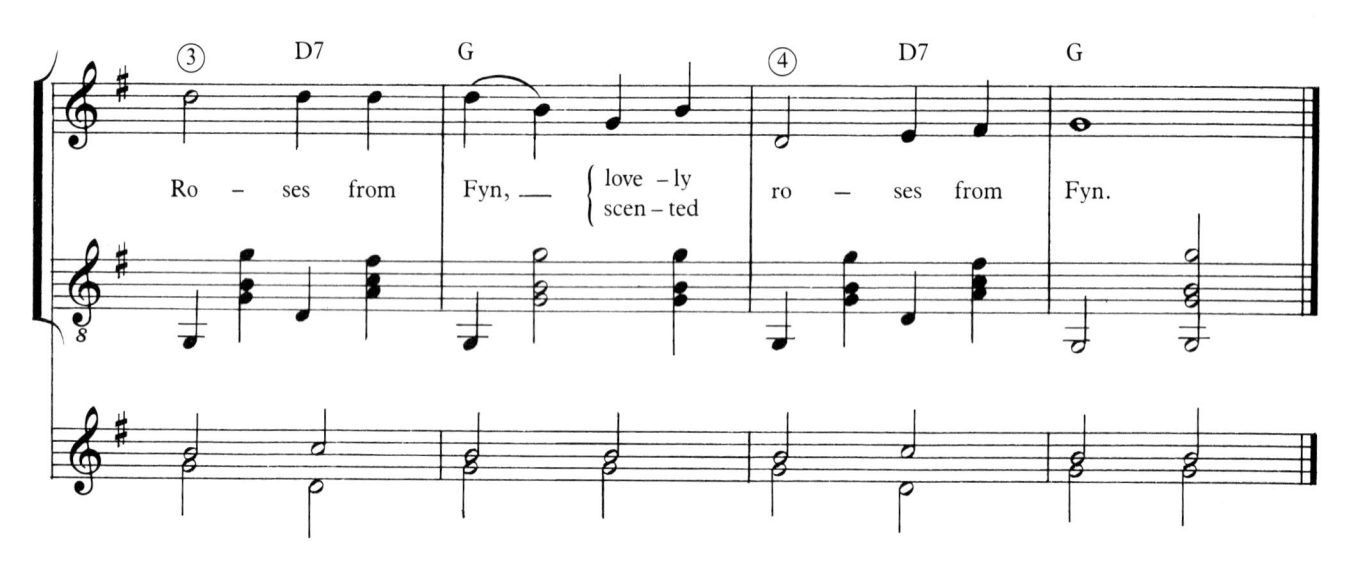

Lyrics: Ro - ses from Fyn. Ro - ses from Fyn. Ro - ses from Fyn, — lovely / scented ro - ses from Fyn.

This very simple four-part round comes from the island birthplace of Hans Christian Andersen. You could alter the words to introduce colours, e.g. 'Roses from Fyn' (*three times*), 'Yellow roses from Fyn', etc.

The descant recorder could play the melody. The chime bar part is very simple (same pattern four times). It could be simpler still if only the lower notes are played. If so, play the 'G' with the R.H. and the 'D' with the L.H. The pattern could be played once before the voices come in as an Introduction and to establish the pitch.

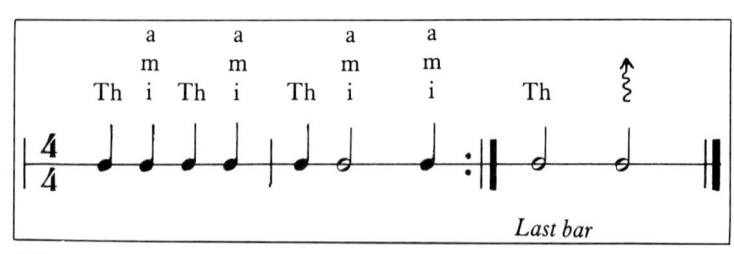

Th i Th i Th i i Th

Last bar

86

Goblin market

Come buy, come buy:
Apples and quinces,
Lemons and oranges,
Plump unpecked cherries,
Melons and raspberries,
Wild free-born cranberries,
Crab-apples, dewberries,
Pineapples, blackberries,
Apricots, strawberries;
All ripe together
In summer weather.

Come buy, come buy:
Our grapes fresh from the vine,
Pomegranates full and fine,
Dates and sharp bullaces,
Rare peaches and greengages,
Damsons and bilberries,
Taste them and try:
Currants and gooseberries,
Bright fire-like barberries,
Figs to fill your mouth,
Citrons from the South,
Sweet to tongue and sound to eye;
Come buy, come buy.

(Extract)

Christina Rossetti

Oh dear, what can the matter be?

With minor word changes this can be developed in different ways. Use the names of your children in the song, each one acting out their own small part. Change 'fair' to store or shop and discuss what each child is going to bring. The 'store' could be the baker's shop, or the butcher's shop, or the newsagent's shop, etc.

With some children, pictures of various objects are useful for stimulation of ideas and these picture (or actual objects) could be 'brought back' from the particular store they went to. Care will also be needed to see that the suggested items fit in rhythmically to the song, e.g.

She/he promised to bring me 'a bag of red apples'.
She/he promised to bring me 'a nice piece of roast beef'.
She/he promised to bring me 'a bright yellow car'.

All sing (perhaps clap on the beat as well) 'Oh dear, what can the matter be', as Johnny goes to the store. Then sing, 'he promised to bring me,' etc. while he selects the object or picture. Finish with the first tune to the words:

Look, look, here he/she comes back again (*three times*)
'Johnny' is back from the store.

I went to visit a farm

Language development
Sequencing

Not fast
Traditional

INTRODUCTION

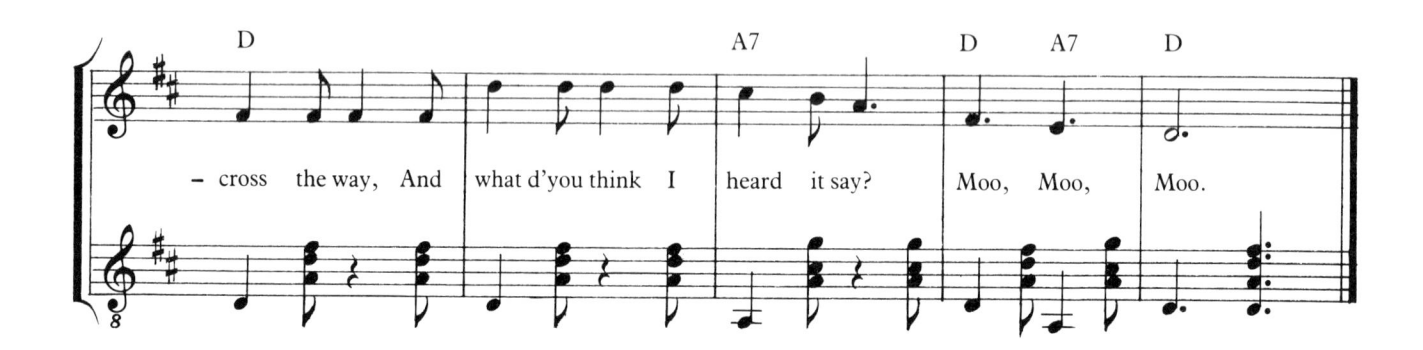

I went to visit a farm one day. I saw a cow across the way, And what d'you think I heard it say? Moo, Moo, Moo.

Repeat using different animals:

e.g. Horse – neigh, neigh, neigh.
    Pig – grunt, grunt, grunt.
    Hen – cluck, cluck, cluck.
                  etc.

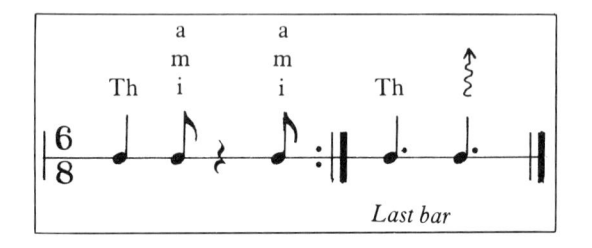

The song can be adapted for a visit to a zoo.

I went to visit a zoo one day.
I saw a bear across the way,
And what d'you think I heard it say,
Growl, growl, growl.

    (*Words: Derek Pearson*)

Snake – hiss, hiss, hiss.
Lions – roar, roar, roar.

The farmyard

One black horse standing by the gate,
Two plump cats eating from a plate;
Three big goats kicking up their heels,
Four pink pigs full of grunts and squeals;
Five white cows coming slowly home.
Six small chicks starting off to roam;
Seven fine doves perched upon the shed,
Eight grey geese eager to be fed.
Nine young lambs full of frisky fun,
Ten brown bees buzzing in the sun.

A. A. Attwood

Horse

The picnickers were sleeping when I,
deciding to be an enormous black horse not seen
in the corner of their field, strolled over.

They had a tartan rug, and a
thermos flask, and they had unwrapped
and eaten little triangles of processed

cheese, with tomatoes. They had been
playing cards among the thistles and
water-biscuits, and had fallen asleep

in the very hot sun. So I was a sudden, black
alarming shadow standing over them, though really
just inquisitive. When one of them heard the
   sound of my breath,

and woke, having dreamt of dragons, and
leapt up and shouted, I had to pretend to
be frightened of them and gallop away.

Alan Brownjohn

The missel-thrush's nest

In early March, before the lark
Dare start, beside the huge oak tree,
Close fixed agen the powdered bark,
The mavis' nest I often see;
And mark, as wont, the bits of wool
Hang round its early bed;
She lays six eggs in colours dull,
Blotched thick with spots of burning red.

John Clare

Incy wincy spider

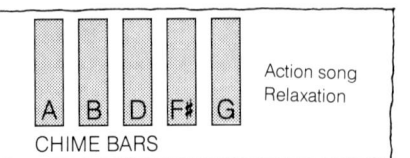

CHIME BARS: A B D F# G

Action song
Relaxation

Traditional

Not fast

INTRODUCTION

CHIME BARS

Incy wincy spider climbed up the water spout. Down came the rain and washed poor Incy out. Out came the sun and dried up all the

90

rain, And In-cy win-cy spi-der climbed up that spout a-gain.

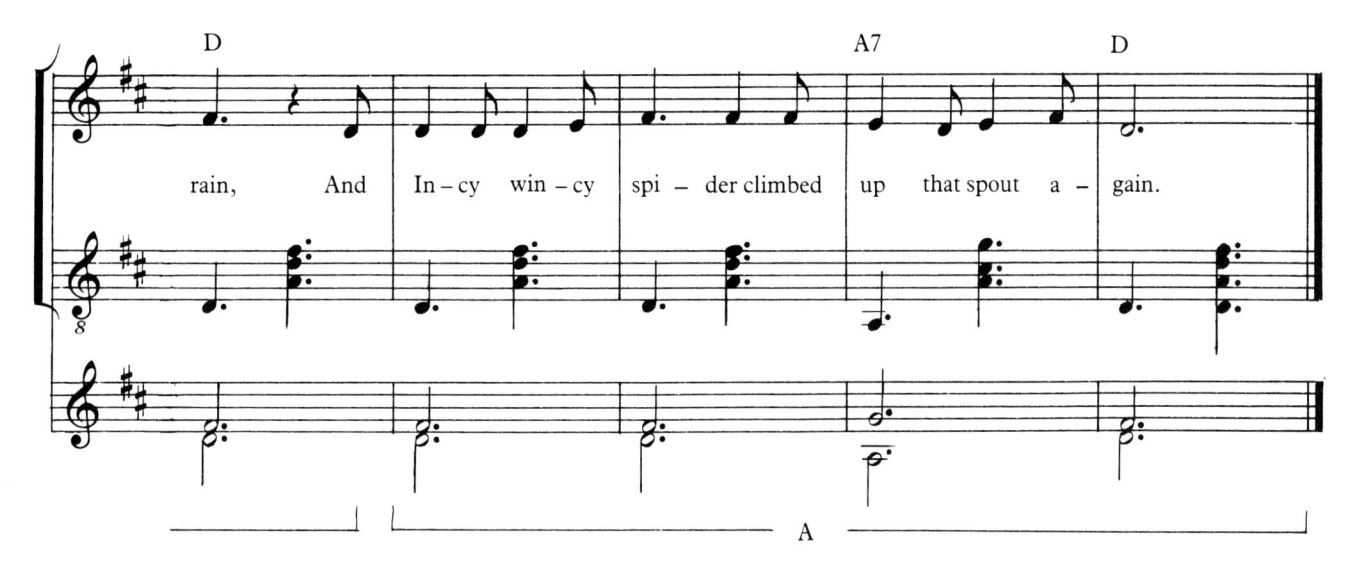

Note the pattern in the chime bar part. The Introduction, first four bars, second four bars, and last four bars are all the same. The remaining four bars should be practised on their own and then fitted in.

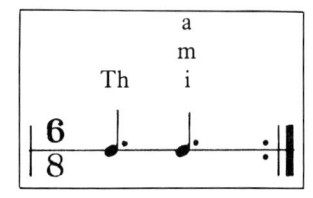

The frugal fly

The frugal fly investigates,
All about my dinner plates;
A crumb that I can hardly see,
Makes a feast for such as he.

John Cunliffe

The spider king

The absent-minded Spider King,
Couldn't quite do anything.
And thro' his web the flies all flew.
For he'd forgot to use the glue.
And when he did, he wasn't clever
He'd get his legs all stuck together.
And falling like a bouncing ball
He'd end up sticking to the wall.
And mutter with exasperation,
'Another sticky situation.'
Whats the fun of being King.
When you can't do anything?

Jeremy Lloyd

Good company

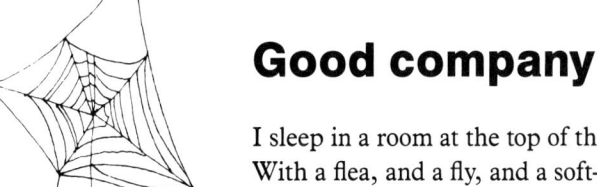

I sleep in a room at the top of the house
With a flea, and a fly, and a soft-scratching mouse,
And a spider who hangs by a thread from the ceiling
Who gives me each day such a curious feeling
When I watch him at work on the beautiful weave
Of his web that's so fine I can hardly believe
It won't all end up in such terrible tangles,
For he sways as he weaves, and spins as he dangles.
I cannot get up to that spider, I know,
And I hope he won't get down to me here below,
And yet when I wake in the chill morning air
I'd miss him if he were not still swinging there,
For I have in my room such good company,
There's him, and the mouse, and the fly, and the flea.

Leonard Clark

Machines

Work in groups (or singly and then combine) and invent a sound to go with a movement to imitate the working parts of a machine. The funnier the vocal sounds the better. Keep it simple at first, but build up the rhythmic, vocal and movement difficulty as confidence increases. (Movements can be tailored to suit those with particular physical problems for therapy and fun.)

Bing Bong Bing Bong

(Arms in and out alternately. Forward and back.)

Inkle Tinkle Inkle Tinkle

(Hands up and down. Move from wrists. Open and close palms and fingers as you go.)

Boom Boom

(Slowly up and down from the knees, standing up straight to start.)

Ump Pump Ssssss

(Alternately, stamp feet (quietly) L, R, then hands high above head on *Sssssss*.)

It is quite likely that an element of pitch will come into this. If so, encourage it.

Engineers

Pistons, valves and wheels and gears
   That's the life of engineers
Thumping, chunking engines going
   Hissing steam and whistles blowing.

There's not a place I'd rather be
   Than working round machinery
Listening to that clanking sound
   Watching all the wheels go round.

Jimmy Garthwaite

Precision

A small red-painted helicopter
buzzes straight and undeviating
overhead.
Rotors clatter,
turning smoothly in pivots of oiled steel.
Bolts, springs, blades, plates,
cool,
efficient,
combine smoothly
and move.
It is guided by man:
this is man's precision.

A small red carrot-fly
(the colour is built-in)
whirrs along an indefinite flight path.
It wings are finely stressed
to the height
of strength and flexibility.
Its built-in guidance system –
a superbly miniaturized computer –
is effectively served
by a wide-angle video-scanner
and twin, highly sensitive antennae.

These combine
to form
an internally guided,
highly manoeuvrable
living flying machine.
God forms it to guide itself;
this is God's precision.

Peter Collenette

Flicker – flicker – flack, flicker – flicker – flack.
The wipers on the car go, flicker – flicker – flack.
The rain goes flick, the rain goes flack.
The wipers on the car go flicker – flicker – flack.
        Flick! Flack!

S. K. Vickery

Traffic lights

Make a mobile with three discs, the colours of traffic lights, on one side, and black on the other side of all three. (Keep the colour sequence from top to bottom as the real traffic lights.)

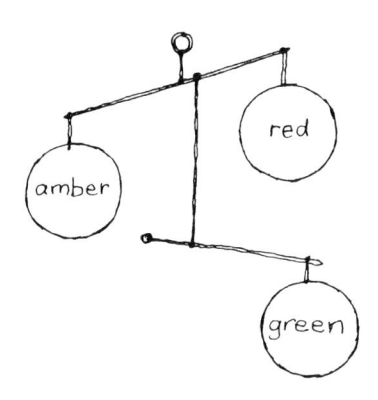

Select, with the children, a colour and an instrument, then discuss what sound pattern they are going to make. Some of the instruments should be pitched and others non-pitched. Sit the children around the mobile and as it rotates the children watch for their colour. When the colour is showing they play their pattern; when the black appears they stop. A refinement is, as the colour starts to appear, to play quietly. When full, play loud and then get quieter as the colour disappears.

These activities could also be recorded to let the children hear and discuss the result. As confidence grows the sound range could include body rhythms and vocal sounds. The more children the greater variety of sounds there are available.

Roar-roaring
Engines running
Horns hooting
Brakes grinding
Gears grating
Rev-revving
Creep, creeping
Overheating
Long waiting
Traffic jam.

Anne English

The city

If you would bottle city songs,
Squeeze them into jars,
Catch the hum of people's voices,
The honk and screech of cars –

If you would capture city sights
And put them with each song,
Seize the beat of walking feet,
And wheels that spin along –

If you would grasp the whirr and blast
Do it fast.

Fog

The fog comes
on little cat feet.
It sits looking
over harbour and city
on silent haunches
and then moves on.

Carl Sandburg

Tommy Thumb

Co-ordination
Action song
Visual awareness

Traditional

Steadily
INTRODUCTION

1. Tom–my Thumb, Tom–my Thumb, Where are you? Here I am, Here I am. How do you do?

2 Peter Pointer, Peter Pointer . . .
3 Toby Tall, Toby Tall . . .
4 Ruby Ring, Ruby Ring . . .
5 Baby Small, Baby Small . . .
6 Fingers All, Fingers All . . .

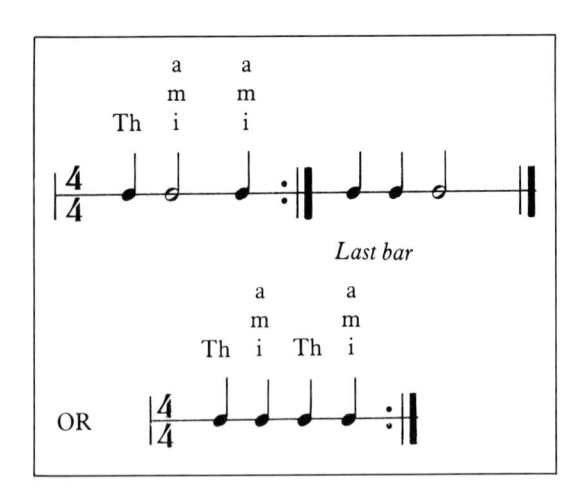

Alternative words

Traffic light, traffic light,
What say you?
I am red, I am red,
You must not go. (Now you must stop!)

Traffic light, Traffic light,
What say you?
Amber now, amber now,
Soon you can go.

Traffic light, traffic light,
What say you?
I am green, I am green,
Now you can go.

There are various sets of words to this tune. Use the set you know and make up others with the children.

Green Train

The Blue Train for the South – but the Green Train for us.
Nobody knows when the Green Train departs.
Nobody sees her off. There is no noise; no fuss;
No luggage on the Green Train;
No whistle when she starts.
But quietly at the right time they wave the green light
And she slides past the platform and plunges into the night.

Wonderful people walking down the long Green Train,
As the engine gathers speed.
And voices talking.
'Where does she go to, Guard?'
Where indeed?
But what does it matter
So long as the night is starred?
Who cares for time, and who cares for the place,
So long as the Green Train thunders on into space?

E. V. Rieu

Use also part, or all, of 'Skimbleshanks, The Railway Cat' by T. S. Eliot, from *Old Possum's Book of Practical Cats*, published by Faber.

The 'local vocal'

Start slowly and quietly. Try to create the feeling of great effort to get the train moving. Gradually get faster, then hold the speed steady.

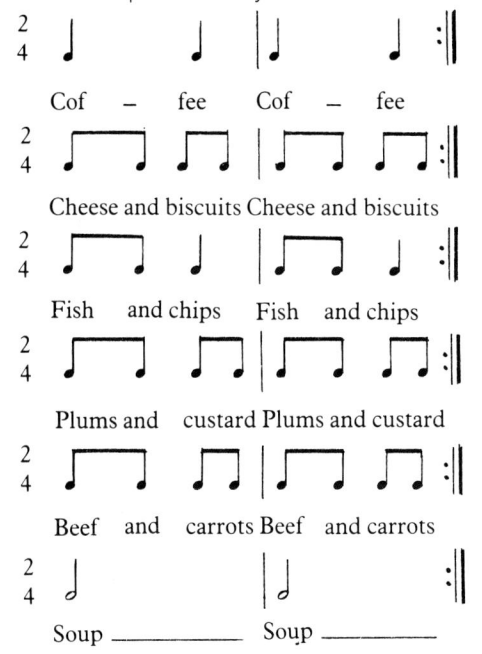

Cof – fee   Cof – fee

Cheese and biscuits Cheese and biscuits

Fish and chips   Fish and chips

Plums and custard Plums and custard

Beef and carrots Beef and carrots

Soup ____   Soup ____

Try to slow it down to a stop again. This can be very difficult to achieve without total collapse.

Thelma the thrush

Thelma the thrush
Made her home in a train.
Just under the engine
To keep out the rain.
Along came the driver
Who said, 'Oh, my word.
I can't move the train
Or I'll frighten the bird.'
Along came the head
Of the railway track.
Who said to the driver,
'I'll give you the sack.
Drive off at once,
You're already late.'
'Not me.' said the driver.
'Nor me.' said his mate,
And smiled down at Thelma
Who looked quite dismayed,
For while they'd been talking
Four eggs had been laid.
'Well, that's it.' said the
Head of the railway track.
'You can't drive off now
Or the eggs will all crack.
I'd best phone the station,
But what shall I say?'
Said the driver, 'The truth.
Uneggspected delay.'

Jeremy Lloyd

Down by the station

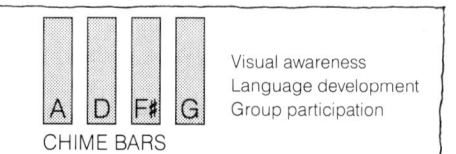

A D F# G
CHIME BARS

Visual awareness
Language development
Group participation

Lively but not too fast   Traditional

INTRODUCTION

sta – tion, ear – ly in the morn – ing. See the lit – tle rail – way trains all in a row. See the en – gine dri – ver pull the lit – tle

96

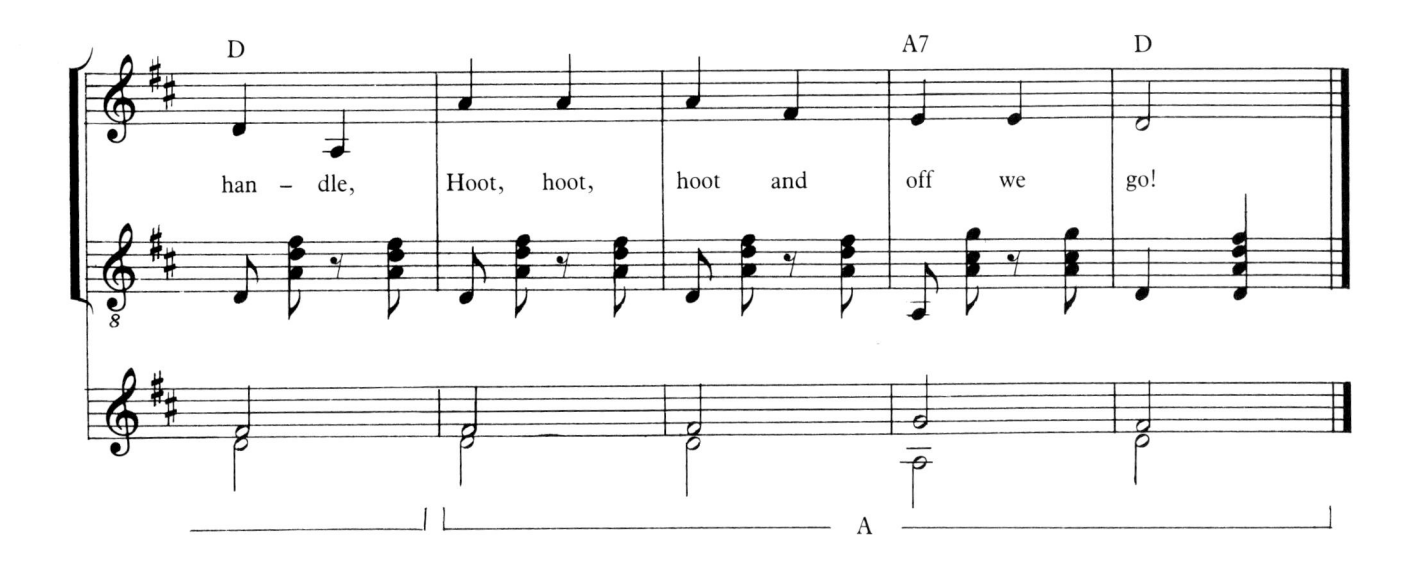

2 Down at the farmyard early in the morning,

See the little tractor standing in the barn
Do you see the farmer turn the little handle?
Chug, chug, chug, and off we go!

3 Down at the garage early in the morning,

See all the buses standing in a row,

Watch the conductor press the little button
Ting, ting, ting, and off we go!

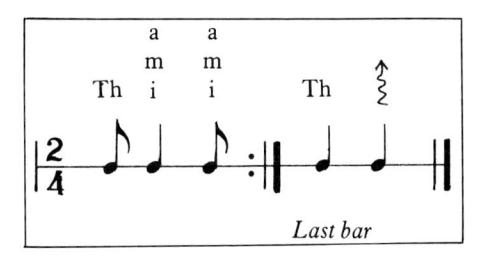

Additional verses

Down by the sea-shore early in the morning
  Walking on the sand all wet and firm.
Quickly take your clothes off, 'Race you to the water.'
  One, two, three and in we go.

Out at the airport early in the morning,
See the great big aeroplanes all in a row.
Can you see the pilot sitting in his cabin?
Engines roar and off they go.

Down at the harbour early in the morning,
Watching all the fishing boats come back from sea.
Lots and lots of boxes, each one filled with fresh fish.
Let's have fish and chips for tea.

(*Words: Derek Pearson*)

(See also *Sing a rainbow*, page 23.)

Morningtown ride

Moderate, with good rhythm

Malvina Reynolds

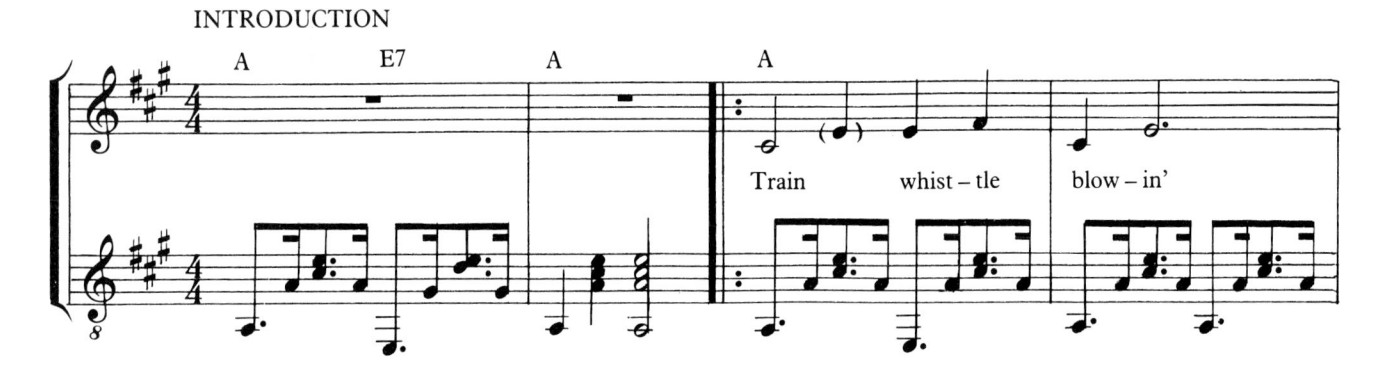

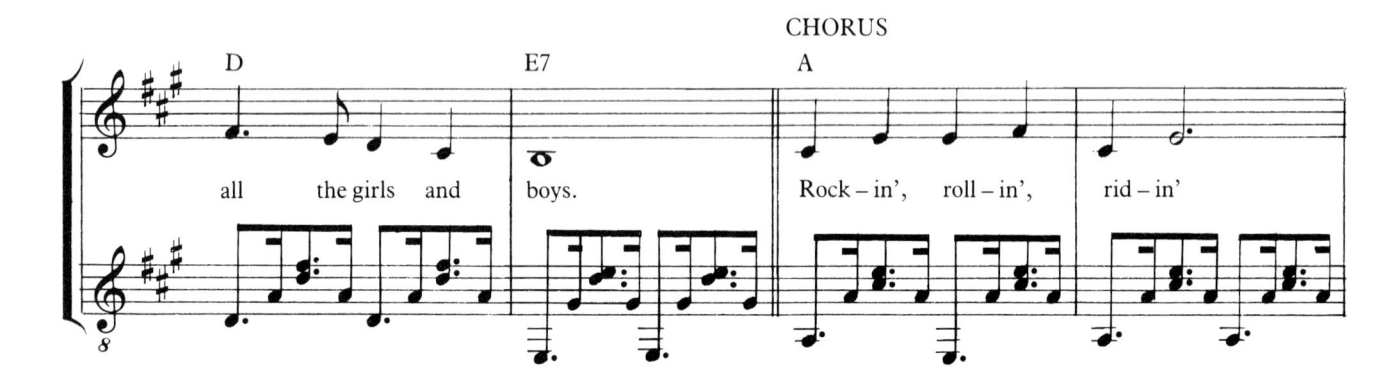

INTRODUCTION

Train whistle blowin' Makes a sleep-y noise; Un-der-neath their blan-kets Go all the girls and boys.

CHORUS

Rock-in', roll-in', rid-in' Out a-long the bay, All bound for Mor-ning-town,

98

```
        E7                    A              Last time
                                             A
Ma-ny    miles    a-way.
```

2 Driver at the engine,
   Fireman rings the bell;
   Sandman swings the lantern
   To say that all is well.

   CHORUS

3 Maybe it is raining,
   Where our train will ride;
   All the little travellers
   Are warm and snug inside.

   CHORUS

4 Somewhere there is sunshine,
   Somewhere there is day;
   Somewhere there is Morningtown,
   Many miles away.

   CHORUS

In verse 2 after the words 'Fireman rings the bell', play the rhythm indicated on an 'A' chime bar or an 'A' on a metallophone.

Fireman rings the bell;

```
       a          a            a           a
                                           m
Th i m i  Th i m i    Th i m i  Th i
                                 Last bar
```

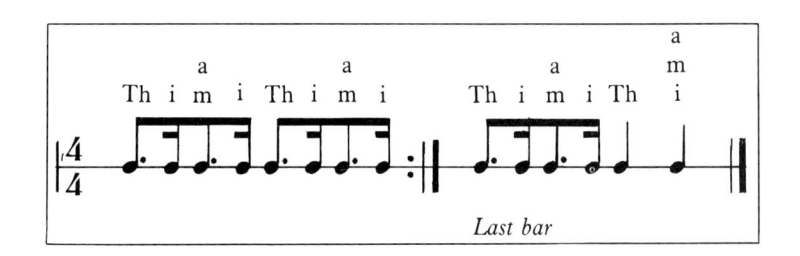

Let's take a ride

Let's take a ride in a big red truck;
Let's take a ride in a streamlined train;
Let's take a ride in a shiny car;
Let's take a ride in an aeroplane.
Just anywhere you want to go,
Any place you want to be,
Choose any way you want to ride,
And come along with me.

Lucille Wood and Louise Scott

Use for creating learning situations.
Colour of truck (red, blue, green, yellow, etc.).
Similar points re train, car, aeroplane.
Where do you want to go? Let's find it.
Can we spell it? Which country is it in?
How do you go? Is it far? Distance?
Simple grammar (a truck, a train, a car, an aeroplane).
Other points as they arise for different groups.

A turkey ran away

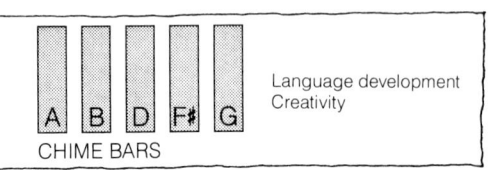

Moderate

INTRODUCTION

Danish folk song
Words: Derek Pearson

1. A turkey ran away, before a Christmas day. Said he, 'They'll make a meal of me, if I should stay!'

2 A nice potato too jumped from the ground and flew,
   Said he, 'They'll roast me through and through if I should stay!'

3 And then a brussels sprout said, 'Now I must get out.
   I'm sure they'll boil my life away if I should stay!'

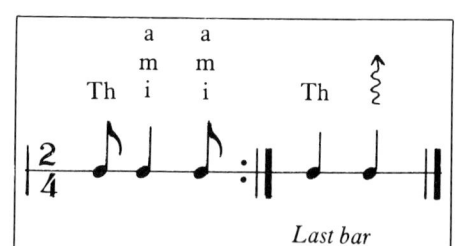

Make up some verses for other seasons or events with the children.

100

Rhythm rhymes

These four rhythm rhymes can be said separately or together. Accentuate the vowel sounds and consonants, e.g. *Soup* – stretch the 'ou' sound with as much relish as possible. This sort of 'fun poem' is good for speech.

'Mix a pancake' can be used on its own for Pancake Tuesday. If possible make pancakes and eat them hot with butter or honey that day. Whether you toss them or not is up to you, your courage and your skill!

These rhymes (or any others you know that will fit) can be done as a Rondo. This is a kind of musical sandwich. First a slice of bread, then a filling, another slice of bread, a different filling, more bread and so on.

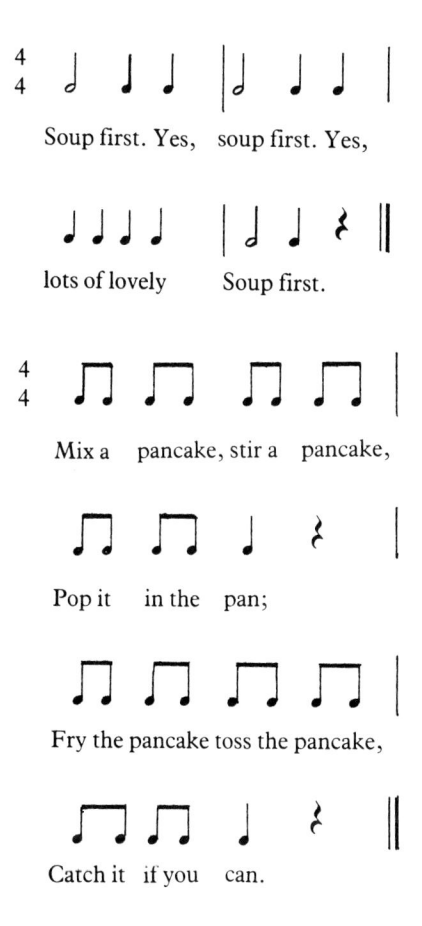

(You could make 'double-decker' sandwiches to illustrate this if possible.) You would build your 'musical sandwich' like this:

Bread – Rhythm rhyme A
Filling – Rhythm rhyme B
Bread – Rhythm rhyme A
Filling – Rhythm rhyme C
Bread – Rhythm rhyme A
Filling – Rhythm rhyme D
Bread – Rhythm rhyme A

The fillings could be in any order, and any rhyme could be the bread.

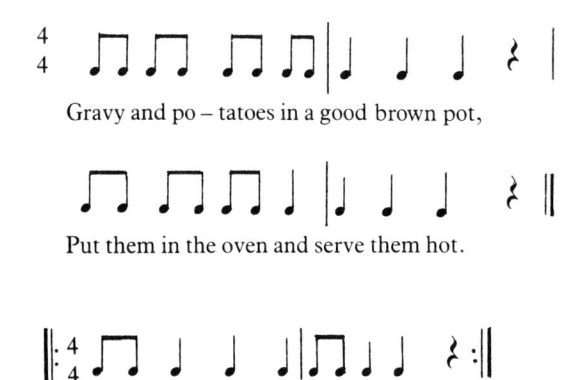

Soup first. Yes, soup first. Yes, lots of lovely Soup first.

Mix a pancake, stir a pancake,
Pop it in the pan;
Fry the pancake toss the pancake,
Catch it if you can.

Gravy and po – tatoes in a good brown pot,
Put them in the oven and serve them hot.

Biscuits and cheese to finish it off.

This rhyme could be used as an alternative to Rhyme 'C' if preferred.

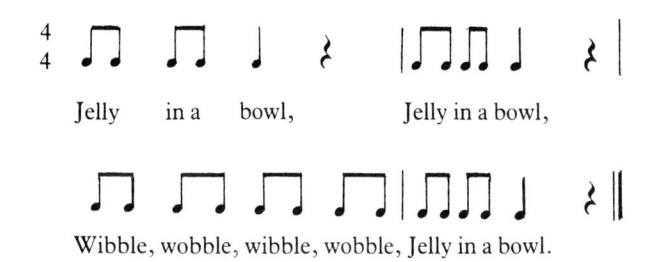

Jelly in a bowl, Jelly in a bowl,
Wibble, wobble, wibble, wobble, Jelly in a bowl.

My sister Lettie

A wonderful thing happened to my sister Lettie,
Instead of hair she grew spaghetti,
And now when she wants a snack at night,
She combs it down and takes a bite.

Manners

I eat my peas with honey
I've done it all my life
It makes the peas taste funny
But it keeps 'em on the knife.

Sing a rainbow

Slowly and simply

Arthur Hamilton

INTRODUCTION

Red and yel-low and pink and green,
Pur-ple and o-range and blue,
I can sing a rain-bow, sing a rain-bow,
Sing a rain-bow too. Lis-ten with your eyes,
Lis-ten with your eyes, And sing ev'ry-thing you see.
You can sing a rain-bow, Sing a rain-bow,

If you only want to sing the first eight bars to start with, play as written but use the rhythm of the very last bar, instead of bar 8, to provide a distinct finish.

OUT FOR THE COUNT

Achievement is vital for everyone, especially those who have frequently failed or been failed. Even such a small thing as being able to count to ten is a real problem. Counting and the use of numbers is involved in so many different activities that it is essential the children can do so with confidence and success. This can be for some a *major* achievement.

One, two, three a-leary *106*
The beehive *108*
Counting song *110*
Flying saucer song *112*
One, two, three, four, five *114*
Pick up a leaf *116*
One more river *118*
The three bears *120*
The chicken song *122*

Copy-count

All sit in a circle. At first the teacher, or leader, claps a number and the first person in the circle claps it back, or taps it on a table or desk. Is it correct? Carry on round the circle.

Later on the children can clap a number and the next person answers. If correct, they then clap to their neighbour, and so on.

This can be varied by using instruments. A xylophone could be used and the children asked to play the number on a *high* note or a *low* note. This helps pitch perception and the high/low concept in sound. It can also be used to help with languages e.g. clap loudly/softly/slowly/quickly. Also for the use of comparatives, e.g. clap more loudly/less loudly; clap more quickly than Alan/ as quickly as Joan/twice as quickly as James, etc. They find out what it all means by doing it. At first it is by doing what you do, but as long as the language is there and clearly linked to the actions, gradually the idea gets across.

The appleman

Hi, hi, hi!
Listen to the cry,
The cry of the Appleman
Passing by:
'Ripe red apple-o,
Nice crisp apple-o,
Try my apple-o,
Buy, buy buy!'

Well, well, well,
Which of you can tell?
How many apples
Did the old man sell?
One on Monday,
Two on Tuesday,
Three on Wednesday,
Four on Thursday,
Five on Friday,
Six on Saturday.
Well, well, well,
Now can you tell? –
How many apples
Did the old man sell?

Helen Clyde

'Top' sounds

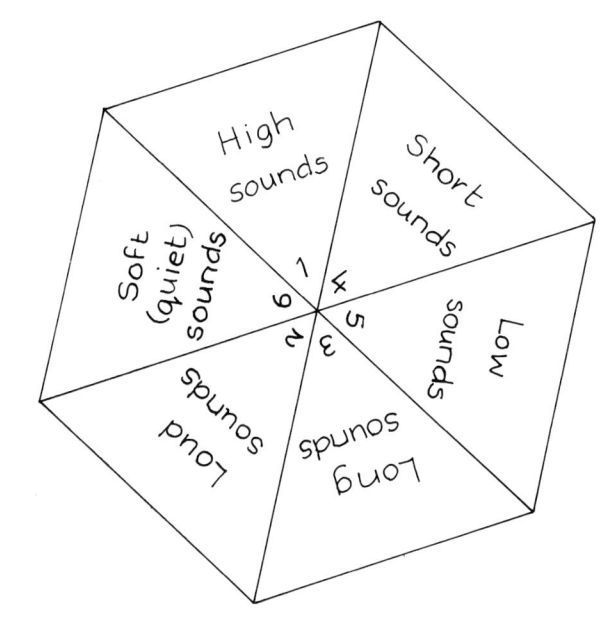

Spin the top and make the sound it gives. Each child does so for their turn. If you find the same 'sound' coming too frequently, spin the top again. Remember the order, then play them all, one after the other, to make a simple composition. Record it on cassette and ask the children to listen carefully and say how they like it? Could they, or would they like to, improve it? How? Why? If so, try again, record again, etc.

Variations

Draw on big cards: hearts – body sounds; clubs – wooden sounds; diamonds – voice sounds; spades – metal sounds. Select one of these cards, add the top sound then create the sound indicated. Record as before. This can give rise to almost endless variations. The recording, listening and discussing teaches the group to listen carefully and take part in group work.

One, two, three a-leary

Not fast, good rhythm Traditional

INTRODUCTION

One, two, three, a-lea-ry, Four, five, six a-lea-ry, Seven, eight, nine, a-lea-ry, Ten a-lea-ry, post-man!

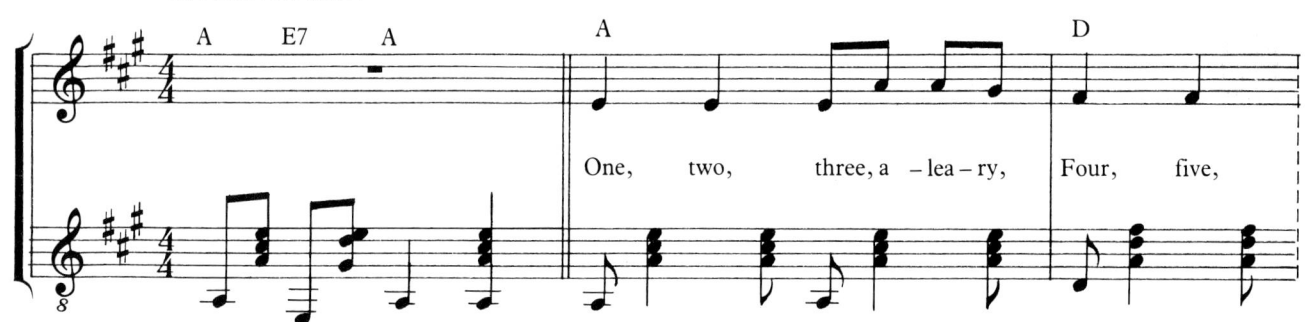

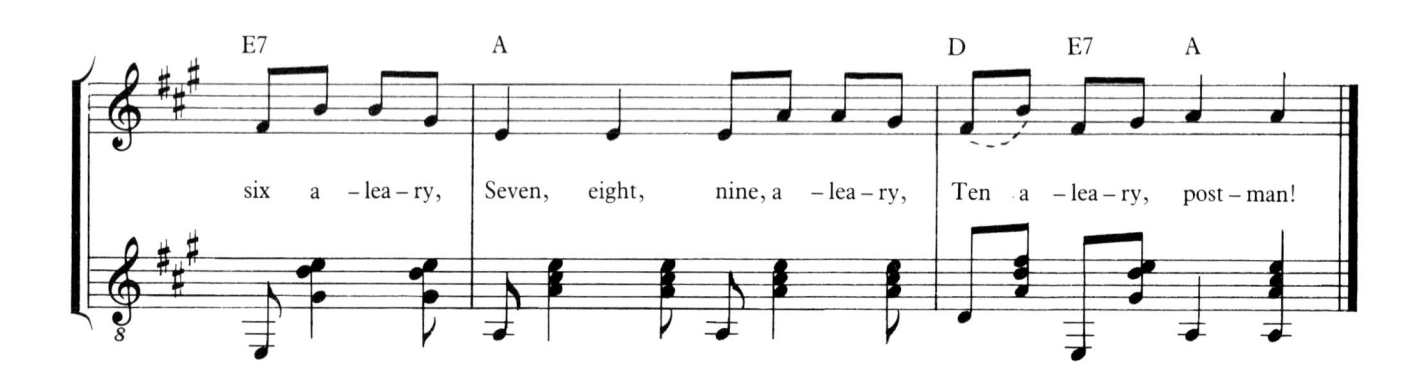

One, two, three, a-twirlsey,
Four, five, six, a-twirlsey,
Seven, eight, nine, a-twirlsey,
Ten a-twirlsey, catch me!

One, two, three, a-jumpsy . . .
One, two, three, a-bouncy . . .

Last bar

The same tune is used for 'In and out the dusky bluebells'.

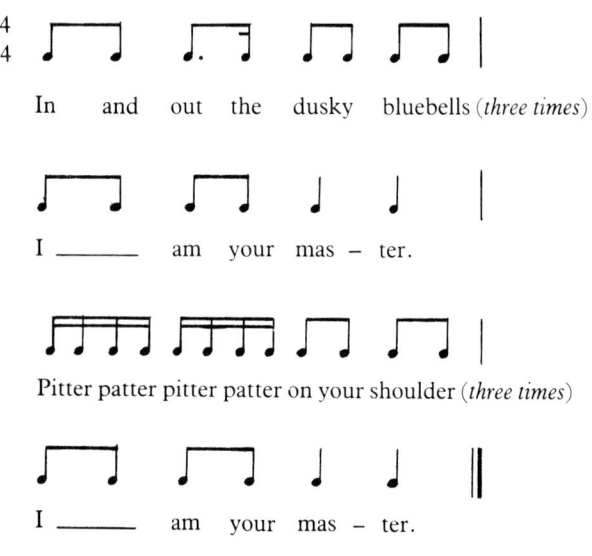

In and out the dusky bluebells (*three times*)

I ____ am your mas - ter.

Pitter patter pitter patter on your shoulder (*three times*)

I ____ am your mas - ter.

The rhythm changes are written with the words. There is no change in the melody.

106

Additional verses

Santa Claus is coming (*three times*) . . .
Now it's almost Christmas.

Hark, I hear the sleigh bells (*three times*) . . .
Jingling on his reindeer.

Nice new dress for Mummy (*three times*) . . .
Just what she was wanting.

Bright red bike for Donald (*three times*) . . .
Yes, it is a racer!

Ho, ho, ho, he's coming (*three times*) . . .
All sing Merry Christmas.

Make up more verses as required; also for other seasons, events or occasions.

(See also 'One potato, two potato, etc.', page 23.)

Twenty-six letters

Twenty-six cards in half a pack;
Twenty-six weeks in half a year;
Twenty-six letters dressed in black
In all the words you ever will hear.

In 'King', 'Queen', 'Ace', and 'Jack',
In 'London', 'lucky', 'lone', and 'lack',
'January', 'April', 'fortify', 'fix',
You'll never find more than twenty-six.

Think of the beautiful things you see
On mountain, riverside, meadow and tree.
How many their names are, but how small
The twenty-six letters that spell them all.

James Reeves

All good children

One, two, three, four, five, six, seven,
All good children go to heaven.
 Some fly east,
 Some fly west,
 Some fly over the cuckoo's nest.

Mincemeat

Sing a song of mincemeat
Currents, raisins, spice,
Apples, sugar, nutmeg,
Everything that's nice.

Stir it with a ladle,
Wish a lovely wish,
Drop it in the middle,
Of your well-filled dish.

Stir again for good luck,
Pack it all away,
Tied in little jars and pots,
Until Christmas Day.

Elizabeth Gould

Can be sung to the tune of 'Sing a song of sixpence', in which case sing first eight lines for verse 1, then repeat first four lines with last four lines added on for verse 2. It is often easier to sing 'Until *it's* Christmas Day' in the last line.

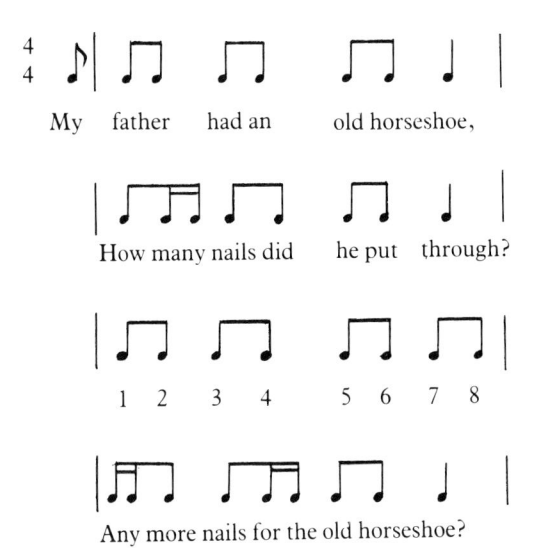

My father had an old horseshoe,

How many nails did he put through?

1 2 3 4 5 6 7 8

Any more nails for the old horseshoe?

Sowing beans

One for the mouse,
One for the crow,
One to rot
And one to grow.

The beehive

Very steady, not fast
INTRODUCTION

Traditional

Lyrics:
This is the bee-hive, where are the bees?
Hidden away where nobody sees.
Out from the hive, out come the bees.
1, 2, 3, 4, 5.

Actions

First six bars. Clench fists, knuckles up, and mark the pulse by moving them up and down. In the last two bars, on 1, 2, 3, 4, 5, bring up fingers one by one. After the song is finished the 'bees' (a few children from the group) could buzz around imitating bee sounds 'zzzzzzz' and then go back to the 'hive', the rest of the group sitting in a circle.

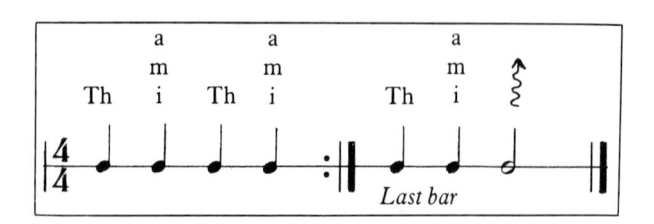

The bass notes of the guitar part could be played on chime bars. Excluding the Introduction, this gives two patterns:

Pattern A D – A – G – D on 'This is the beehive, where are the bees?', and 'Out from the hive, out come the bees'.

Pattern B G – D – A – D on 'Hidden away where nobody sees', and '1, 2, 3, 4, 5.'

The Introduction would be D – A – D – D.

It is essential to have the low-pitch chime bars to play this at the desired pitch level.

The bumble bee

The bumble bee is oddly wrought
Aerodynamically it ought
To find it quite impossible to rise
But bumble bees don't know the rule,
For bumble bees don't go to schule –
They flies.

Joyce Grenfell

One, Two, Three,
The bumble bee.
The rooster crows,
And away she goes!

(See also 'The farmyard', page 89)

Farmer Jackson's farm

Farmer Jackson has on his farm:
    one dog
    two cats
    three goats
    four pigs
    five hens
    six cows
    seven geese
    eight ducks
    nine sheep
    ten lambs
– and hidden away where nobody sees,
a hundred hundred honey-bees!

Clive Sansom

Picture bricks

Select a picture that has some bold, clear feature(s). This will have to be in relation to the age and ability of the children. The ideal size is about 6″ by 8″ (150 mm×200 mm) or larger. Take three lengths (more if required for width) of 2″ by 2″ (50 mm× 50 mm) wood and clamp together. Glue the picture onto the wood and when dry mark through the picture, with a very sharp knife, into 2″ squares. Varnish with clear polyurethane varnish (two or three coats.). Carefully cut the lengthwise joins of the picture; then, with a fine saw cut into 2″ cubes. (This can often be done for you in the woodwork room of the local secondary school or technical college.) Carefully sandpaper the rough sides, seal and paint in bright colours. Add numbers or letters if you like.

Use as a brick jigsaw and invent games. Many variations on this are possible and the range can be adapted to suit any age level. It is usually best with the younger or lower ability children. If you put a picture on the front and on the back you extend the possibilities. Pictures front and back, numbers and bold plain colours on the sides and you have a simply made but very useful educational toy.

Counting song

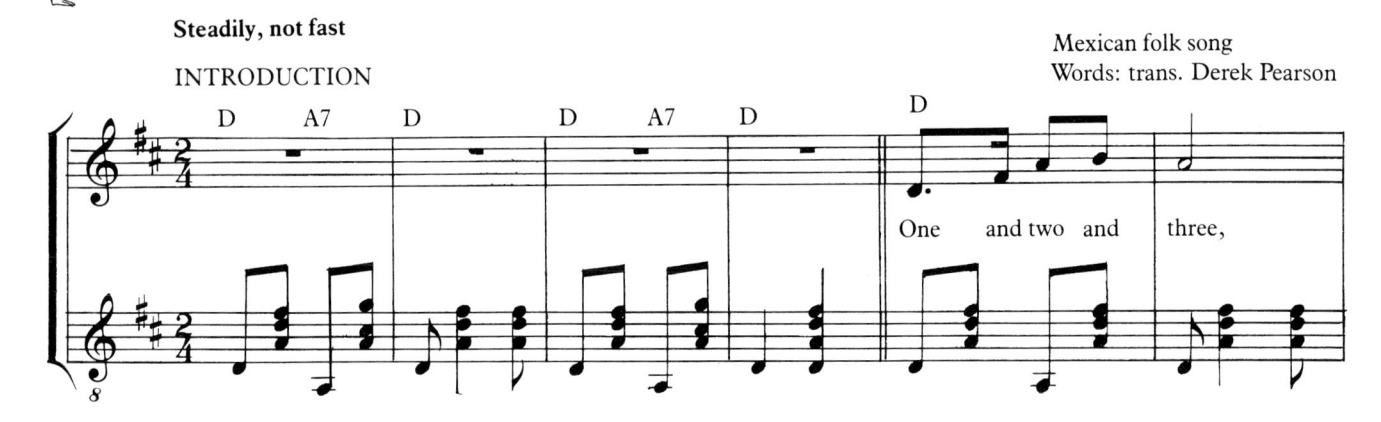

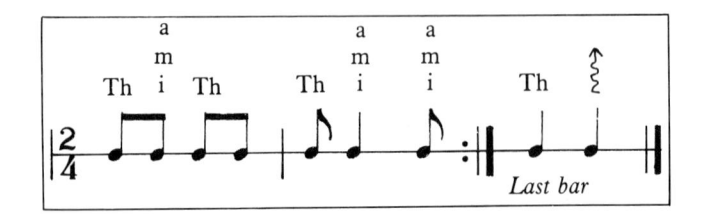

Steadily, not fast

INTRODUCTION

Mexican folk song
Words: trans. Derek Pearson

One and two and three, Four and five and six, Se – ven eight and nine, There now I can count to ten.

La la la la la, la la la la la, la la la la la la. la.

(See also 'The grocers', later in this section on page 113.)

110

The apple-tree

On the farmer's apple-tree,
Five red apples I can see.
Some for you, some for me –
Eat one apple from the tree.

On the farmer's apple-tree,
Four red apples I can see.
Some for you, some for me –
Eat one apple from the tree . . .

Dorothy Williams

Make an apple-tree in card, and some apples that you can stick on with Blu-tak or similar material. As each verse is said one of the children goes and 'picks' an apple, then everyone counts how many are left. The poem could just as easily start at 'ten red apples.' The well known felt-board or flannel-graph would be equally effective here, and simple for the children to use.

The merle and the blackbird

The merle and the blackbird,
The laverock and the lark,
The plover and the lapwing –
How many birds is that?

(Three: each line is two names for the same bird.)

Old Man Moon

The moon is very, very old.
The reason is quite clear –
He gets a birthday once a month,
Instead of once a year.

Aileen Fisher

A dozen is twelve

A dozen is twelve,
Or four times three.
Half a dozen is six,
As plain as can be.

Using wooden bricks, balls, oranges, etc. lay out the patterns as mentioned in the rhyme. Can the children find any other patterns that add up to twelve? Expand in similar vein.

A counting rhyme

One little,
Two little,
Three little pigs,
Small and fat and pink,
Fell into a tub of tar
And turned as black as ink.
Four little,
Five little,
Six little pigs
Went to see the moon;
They found it colder than they thought,
And came back very soon.
Seven little,
Eight little,
Nine little pigs
Went to look for gold;
They found it in a pickle-jar,
At least, that's what I'm told.

M. M. Stephenson

Porridge for one,
Porridge for two,
I shall be done long
Long before you.

Flying saucer song

Moderate — Traditional

INTRODUCTION

CHIME BARS: A D F# G

Ten little men in flying saucers
Flew round the world one day.
They looked left and right,
But they did-n't like the sight,
So one man flew a-way.

Nine little men in flying saucers . . .
Eight little men in flying saucers . . .

to:

One little man in a flying saucer,
Flew round the world one day.
He looked left and right,
But he didn't like the sight,
So then he flew away.

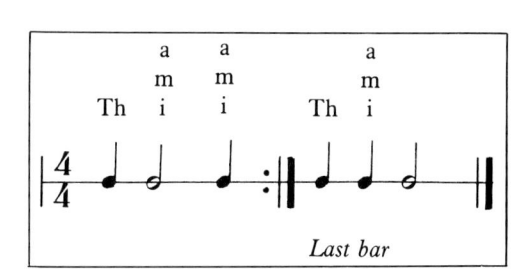

The descant recorder could play the melody.

See also 'We're ten miles from home' sung to the tune of 'Walking to the town', page 18. It makes a good action and counting song.

The grocers

One grocer worked hard weighing rice,
Two grocers worked hard packing spice,
Three grocers worked hard sorting teas,
Four grocers worked hard wrapping cheese.
Five grocers worked hard stacking jam,
Six grocers worked hard slicing ham,
Seven grocers worked hard cutting meats,
Eight grocers worked hard opening sweets,
Nine grocers worked hard selling bread,
Ten grocers, tired out, went home to bed.

Barbara Ireson

Engine, engine, number nine,
Sliding down Chicago line.
When she's polished she will shine
Engine, engine, number nine.

Engine, engine, number nine,
Dipped her nose in turpentine.
Turpentine will make it shine
Engine, engine, number nine.

Six times one

Is six times one a lot of fun?
Or eight times two?
Perhaps for you.
But five times three
Unhinges me,
While six times seven and eight times eight
Put me in an awful state
And four and six and nine times nine
Make me want to cry and whine
So when I get to twelve times ten
I begin to wonder when
I can take a vacation from multiplication
And go out
And start playing again.

Karla Kuskin

P.C. Plod at the pillar box

It's snowing out
streets are thiefproof
A wind that blows
straight up your nose
no messin
A night
not fit to be seen with a dog
out in

On the corner
P.C. Plod (brave as a mountain lion)
passes the time of night
with a pillar box
'What's 7 times 8 minus 56?'
he asked mathematically
The pillar box was silent for a moment
and then said
nothing
'Right first time,'
said the snowcapped cop
and slouched off towards Bethlehem
Avenue

Roger McGough

Counting cherry stones

One, two, three, four,
Mary at the cottage door,
Five, six, seven, eight,
Eating cherries off a plate.

Tinker, tailor, soldier, sailor,
Rich man, poor man, beggar man, thief.

(Counting the stones to tell the future!)

Hickory, dickory 6 and 7.
Alabone, crackabone 10 and 11.
Spin, spun must be done
Twiddle'um, twaddle'um 21,
O – U – T spells out.

One, two, three, four, five

Good rhythm, not fast
Traditional

INTRODUCTION

One two three four five, Once I caught a fish a-live,

Six seven eight nine ten, Then I let it go a-gain. Why did you let it go? Be-

-cause he bit my fin-ger so. Which fin-ger did he bite? This lit-tle fin-ger on the right.

Last bar

OR

The storm

First there were two of us, then there were three of us,
Then there was one bird more,
Four of us – wild white sea-birds,
Treading the ocean floor;
And the wind rose, and the sea rose,
To the angry billows' roar –
With one of us – two of us – three of us – four of us
Sea-birds on the shore.

Soon there were five of us, soon there were nine of us,
And lo! in a trice sixteen!
And yeasty surf curdled over the sands,
And gaunt grey rocks between;
And the tempest raved, and the lightning's fire
Struck blue on the sprindrift hoar –
And on four of us – ay, and on four times four of us
Sea-birds on the shore.

And our sixteen waxed to thirty-two,
And they to past three score –
A wild, white welter of winnowing wings,
And ever more and more;
And the winds lulled, and the sea went down,
And the sun streamed out on high,
Gilding the pools and the spume and the spars
'Neath the vast blue deeps of the sky.

And the isles and the bright headlands shone,
As they'd never shone before.
Mountains and valleys of silver cloud,
Wherein to swing, sweep, soar –
A host of screeching, scolding, scrabbling
Sea-birds on the shore –
A snowy, silent, sun-washed drift
Of sea-birds on the shore.

Walter de la Mare

Pick up a leaf

Steadily, not fast

INTRODUCTION

Tune: traditional
Words: Lucille Wood

CHIME BARS: D G B C

1. Pick up a leaf and put it in a bas-ket,
Pick up a leaf and put it in a bas-ket,
Pick up a leaf and put it in a bas-ket,
Yel-low red and brown.

2. I found a leaf and put it in my basket,
   I found a leaf and put it in my basket,
   I found a leaf and put it in my basket,
   Yellow, red and brown.

3. How many leaves do you have in your basket?
   How many leaves do you have in your basket?
   How many leaves do you have in your basket?
   1, 2, 3, 4, 5.

The descant recorder could play the melody.

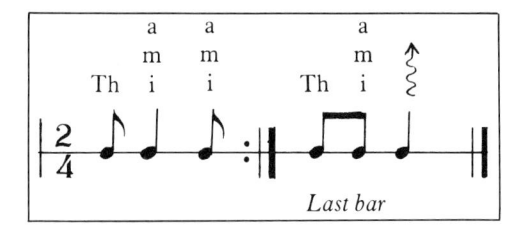

Using the tune of 'Pick up a leaf':

Sit on the chair, it's very nearly lunchtime . . .
  We are very hungry.

Lie on the bed and have a little rest now . . .
  We all feel so sleepy.

Stand in the shower and wash yourself all over . . .
  Oh, it's really lovely.

Lie on the sand and watch the people swimming . . .
  Look here comes a big boat.

Look at the man, he's under the red car.
  He will mend it quickly.

Language comprehension and its expressive use can be reinforced by using songs and fitting suitable sets of words to them. Spatial relationships involving bodily movement have verbal instructions which are given greater meaning by repetition in different ways e.g. the prepositions *on*, *in*, *under*. Expand to suit the needs of the children.

Pocket board

Using a pocket board (or similar idea) make phrase cards associated with the ideas in the song and use to extend the children's experience, e.g.

| Pick up a | leaf |

Use first as it stands, then insert the colour of the leaf, on a separate card, e.g.

| red | green |

This can be developed in many ways:

| Pick up | five | leaves |

| Pick up | five | red | leaves |

As the song is sung the children can mime picking up leaves. Substitute 'leaf' with other words and turn into a game. Many 'variations on the theme' can be devised to hold the children's attention and develop language and other skills e.g. name empty boxes with the various colours of the leaves, and have a large number of real or paper leaves for the children to sort out into the correct box. (Extend to other songs.)

Holes of green

Trees are full of holes –
between the leaves, I mean;
but if you stand away enough
the holes fill up with green.

One log won't burn,
Two logs may,
Three logs *must* burn
And four will blaze away.

One more river

Steady, with good rhythm

Traditional American

INTRODUCTION

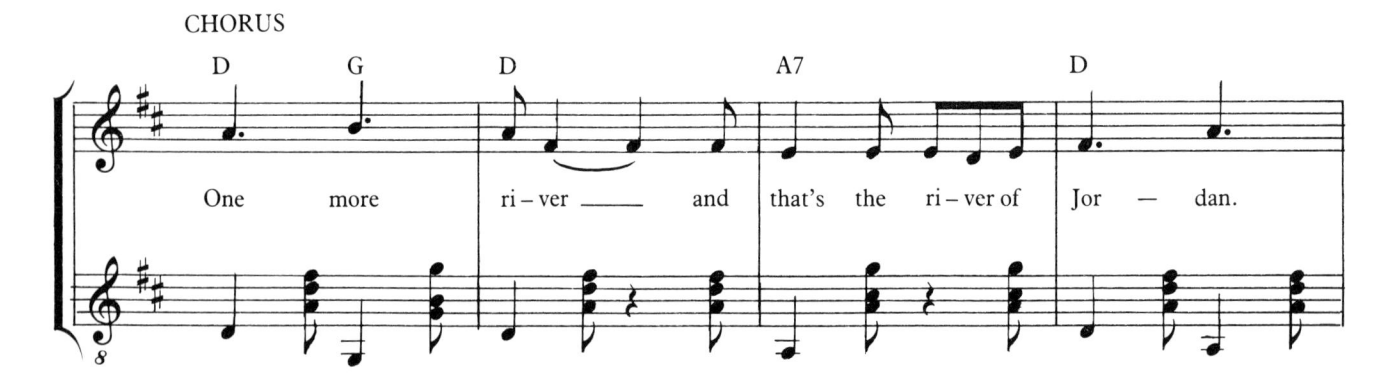

1. Old No-ah once he built an ark, There's one more ri-ver to cross. And patched it up with Hicko-ry bark, There's one more ri-ver to cross.

CHORUS

One more ri-ver ____ and that's the ri-ver of Jor — dan.

One more ri-ver, ____ There's one more ri-ver to cross.

2. The animals went in one by one,
   There's one more river to cross.

   The elephant chewing a caraway bun,
   There's one more river to cross.

3. The animals went in two by two . . .

   The rhinoceros and the kangaroo . . .

4. The animals went in three by three . . .

   The bear, the flea and the bumble bee . . .

5. The animals went in four by four . . .

   Old Noah got mad and hollered for more . . .

6. The animals went in five by five . . .

   Let's hope we can keep them all alive . . .

7. The animals went in six by six . . .

   The hyena laughed at the monkey's tricks . . .

8. The animals went in seven by seven . . .

   Said the cat to the elephant, 'Who are you shovin?'

9. The animals went in eight by eight . . .

   Noah cried, 'Quick, I'm closing the gate.' . . .

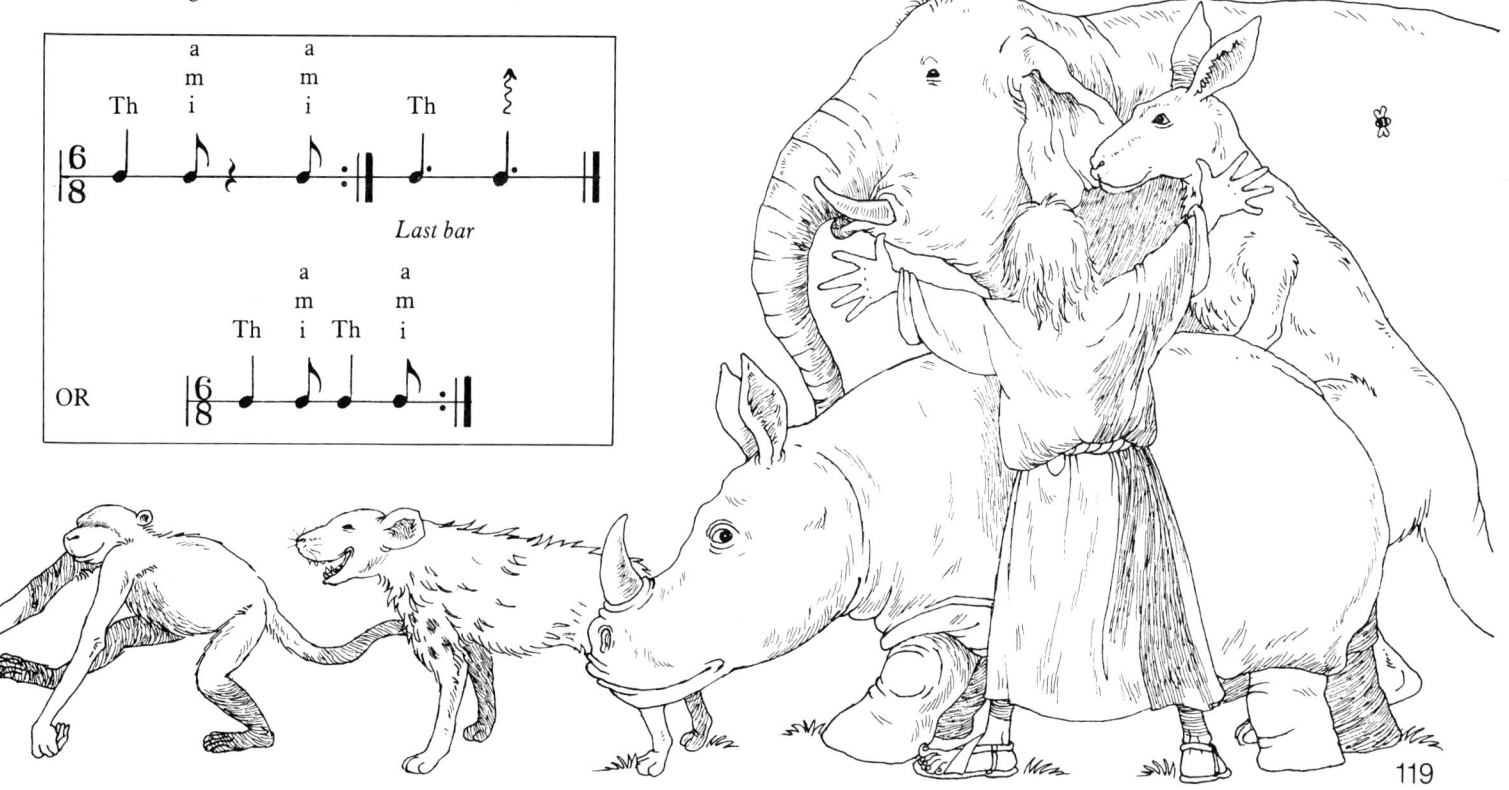

The three bears

Moderate, with good swinging rhythm

INTRODUCTION

Tune: traditional
Words: Carolyn S. Bailey

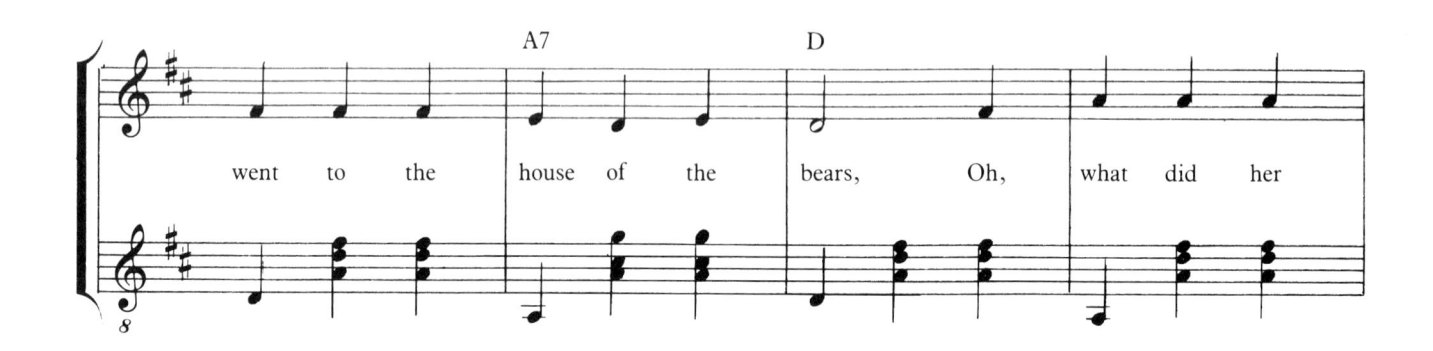

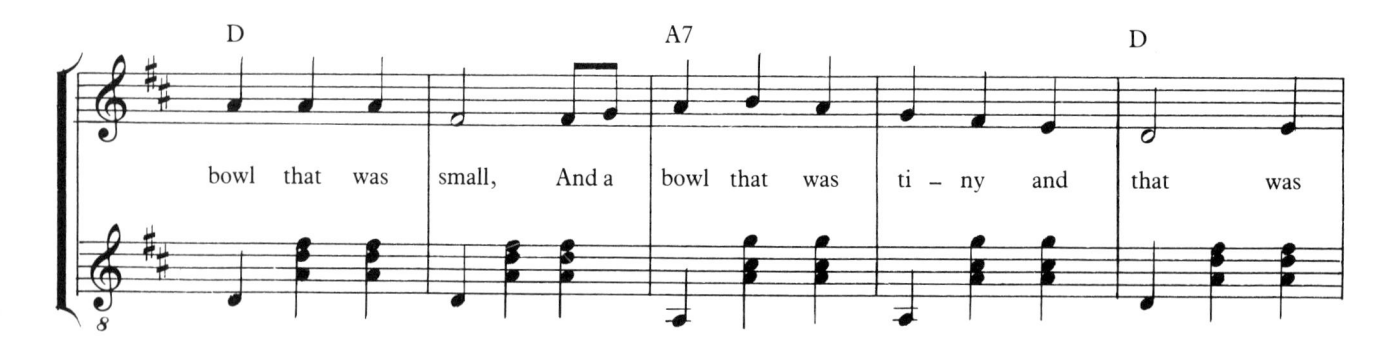

1. When Goldilocks went to the house of the bears, Oh, what did her blue eyes see? A bowl that was huge, A bowl that was small, And a bowl that was tiny and that was

all, She count-ed them one two three.

2. When Goldilocks went to the house of the bears,
   Oh, what did her blue eyes see?
   A chair that was huge . . .

3. When Goldilocks went to the house of the bears,
   Oh, what did her blue eyes see?
   A bed that was huge . . .

4. When Goldilocks went to the house of the bears,
   Oh, what did her blue eyes see?
   A bear that was huge
   A bear that was small
   And a bear that was tiny, and that was all,
   They growled at her, grr, grr, grr.

In 'The three bears', add sounds and actions to the text. On 'Gold' of Goldilocks play a 'D' on a high pitch chime bar or glockenspiel. Every time the bears are mentioned play a moderately loud note on a low pitch drum. For 'blue eyes see', point to their eyes and then all round. When in each verse we have 'A bowl (etc.) that was huge . . . small . . . tiny', hold their arms out wide . . . medium . . . then hands out close together. At 'One, two, three', count out on their fingers, or hold up 1-2-3 fingers as they sing. These are only suggestions and should be altered or added to as is necessary to suit your children.

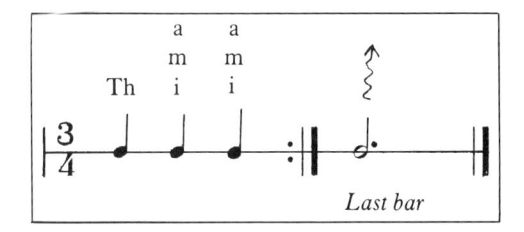

The chicken song

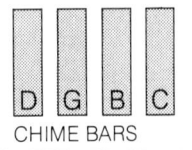

Not fast, good rhythm

Traditional

CHIME BARS: D G B C

INTRODUCTION

CHIME BARS

1. Said the first little chicken with a queer little squirm, 'I wish I could find a fat little worm'.

CHORUS

'Now see here', said the mother from the green garden patch, 'If you want any breakfast, Just scratch, scratch scratch.'

2 Said the next little chicken
　With an odd little shrug,
　'I wish I could find
　A fat little slug'.

3 Said the third little chicken
　With a sharp little squeal,
　'I wish I could find
　Some nice yellow meal'.

4 Said the fourth little chicken

　With a sigh of grief,
　'I wish I could find

　A little green leaf.'

5 Said the fifth little chicken
　With a faint little moan,
　'I wish I could find
　A wee gravel stone'.

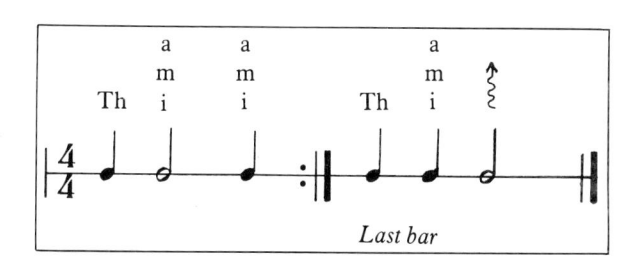

Last bar

Eggs are laid by turkeys

Eggs are laid by turkeys
Eggs are laid by hens
Eggs are laid by robins
Eggs are laid by wrens
Eggs are laid by eagles
Eggs are laid by quail,
Pigeons, parrots, peregrines;
And that's how every bird begins.

Chook-chook

Chook, chook, chook-chook-chook!
Good morning, Mrs Hen.
How many chickens have you got?
Madam, I've got ten.
Four of them are yellow,
And four of them are brown,
And two of them are speckled red,
The nicest in the town.

Mary Ann Hobermann

One snail, two snails

One snail and two snails
Had a little talk;
One snail and two snails
Went a little walk.
They came to a garden
And climbed up a tree,
Where a jolly kookaburra
Gobbled up all three.

Mary Gilmore

HERE, THERE AND EVERYWHERE

This is a short and more general section with the balance weighted slightly towards older children. It should allow the introduction of conceptual and social ideas if and where the children are ready to understand them as well as the established patterns used and evolved in earlier material. Don't miss the many possibilities for dramatizing songs and poems in this section, some just by the addition of simple sound effects and movements, others by what could amount to a fairly extravagant form of production. This can help them enter the magic world of make-believe. Many children need help and encouragement, but once given this can amaze us with their reactions to life, events, attitudes to others and emotions or personal feelings towards things. The development of the ability to sustain a complete story is an important achievement for many children.

Going to the zoo   *126*
Wiggley Woo   *128*
Apple song   *130*
The ink is black   *132*
Puff the magic dragon   *134*
Nellie the elephant   *138*
Popeye the sailor man   *140*
Up, up and away   *142*

Going to the zoo

CHORUS   When we have a holiday
Oh, what shall we do?
We'll take a little bus ride
And go to the zoo.

We like the monkeys best of all,
We like the way they jump.
They climb up high with hands and feet,
And sometimes slide down bump!

The elephant is big and strong,
Just watch what he can do.
He'll take a penny in his trunk
And ring a bell for you.

The giraffe has such a long, long neck,
He stretches up so high
To reach the top leaves on the tree.
He seems to touch the sky.

The sea-lions lie beside their pool,
They look around to see
The keeper coming with the fish
He brings them for their tea.

The kangaroos stand very still,
Just looking all around,
Then suddenly away they go,
All leaping off the ground.

     from *Poems for Movement* (Evans)

Chameleon

I can think sharply
and I can change:
my colours cover a considerable range.

I can be some mud by
an estuary,
I can be a patch on the bark of a tree.

I can be green grass
or a little thin stone
– or if I really want to be left alone,

I can be a shadow . . .
What I am on your
multi-coloured bedspread, I am not quite sure.

     Alan Brownjohn

Norman the zebra

Norman, a zebra at the zoo,
Escaped and ran to Waterloo
And caused a lot of consternation,
In the rush-hour, at the station.
He had an awful lot of fun
Chasing folk on Platform 1.
And then he ran to Regent's Park
And hid there until it was dark.
And thought of his keeper Mr Prout.
How cross he'd be, that he'd got out.
So he tiptoed to the big zoo gate
And found he'd got there just too late.
Poor Norman had a little weep
And lay down in the road to sleep
And woke up early from his rest,
With people walking on his chest.
And someone said. 'I think that's new.
A zebra crossing near the zoo.'
And with a snort of indignation.
Regretting leaving for the station,
He cried, 'I've had enough of that,
How dare you use me as a mat.
I'm going straight home to the zoo.'
He was just in time for breakfast too.

     Jeremy Lloyd

Cousin Nell
married a frogman
in the hope
that one day
he would turn into
a handsome prince.

Instead he turned into
a sewage pipe
near Gravesend
and was never seen again.

     Roger McGough

Use also 'The Zoo' by Boris Pasternak translated by Lydia Pasternak in *A flock of words* (The Bodley Head). This is a longish poem but it can be used in sections and is different, in an interesting way, from most Zoo poems. Pasternak has also written 'Christmas Star' (same collection) another poem which again provides a different slant, this time on the Nativity.

Going to the zoo

Steadily, with lively rhythm

Tom Paxton

INTRODUCTION

2 See the elephant with the long trunk swingin'
Great big ears and long trunk swingin'
Sniffin' up peanuts with the long trunk swingin'
We can stay all day.
CHORUS

3 Big black bear all huff huff a-puffin'
Coat's too heavy, he's huff huff a-puffin'
Don't get too near the huff huff a-puffin'
Or you won't stay all day.
CHORUS

With younger children use pictures of the various animals and, if possible, visit a zoo. What other animals do you find in zoos? Why? Act out how the animals might move as suggested in the song.

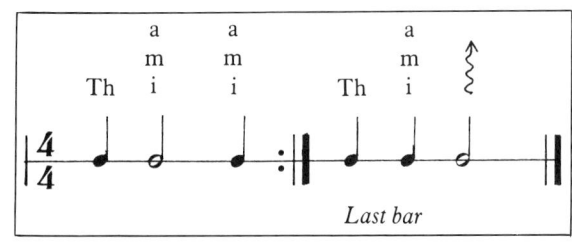

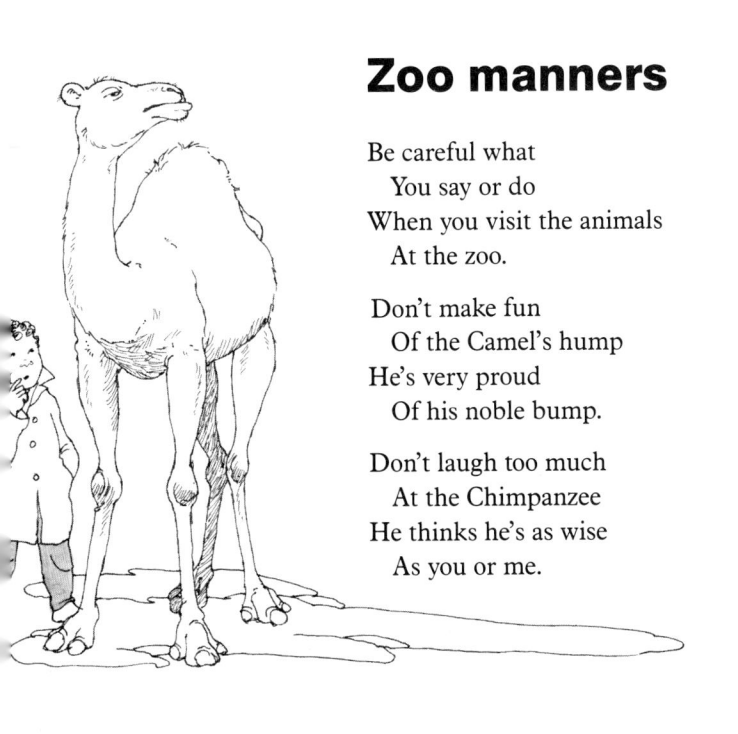

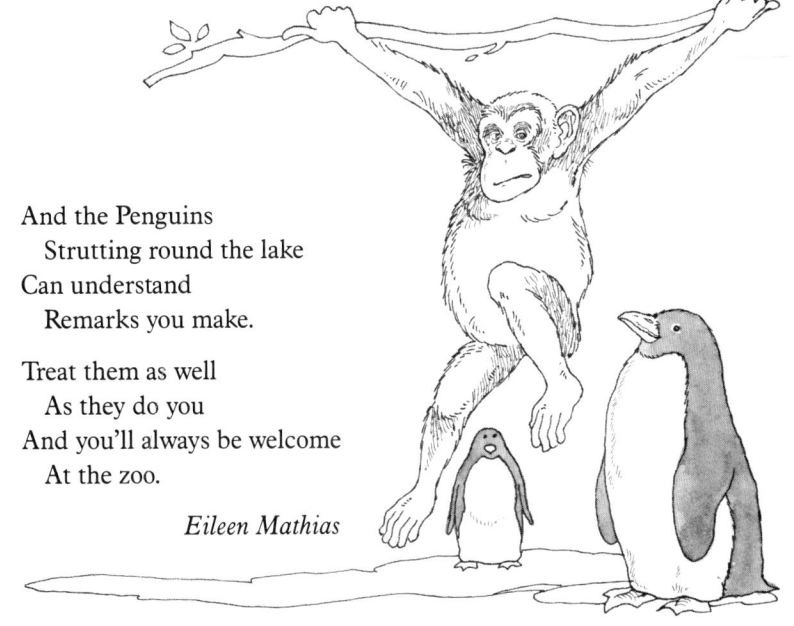

4 See all the monkeys scritch scritch scratchin'
Jumpin' all around and scritch scritch scratchin'
Hangin' by their long tails scritch scritch scratchin'
We can stay all day.
CHORUS

5 Seals in the pool all honk honk honkin'
Catchin' fish and honk honk honkin'
Little seals all honk honk honkin' (*high pitched voice*)
We can stay all day.
CHORUS

Zoo manners

Be careful what
   You say or do
When you visit the animals
   At the zoo.

Don't make fun
   Of the Camel's hump
He's very proud
   Of his noble bump.

Don't laugh too much
   At the Chimpanzee
He thinks he's as wise
   As you or me.

And the Penguins
   Strutting round the lake
Can understand
   Remarks you make.

Treat them as well
   As they do you
And you'll always be welcome
   At the zoo.

Eileen Mathias

Wiggley Woo

Not fast   Traditional

INTRODUCTION

There's a worm at the bot-tom of my gar-den, And his name is Wig-gle-y Woo. There's a worm at the bot-tom of my gar-den, And all that he can do, Is wig-gle all day and wig-gle all night, The neigh-bours say he's a ter-ri-ble fright, There's a worm at the bot–tom of my gar–den, And his name is Wig–gle–y Woo.

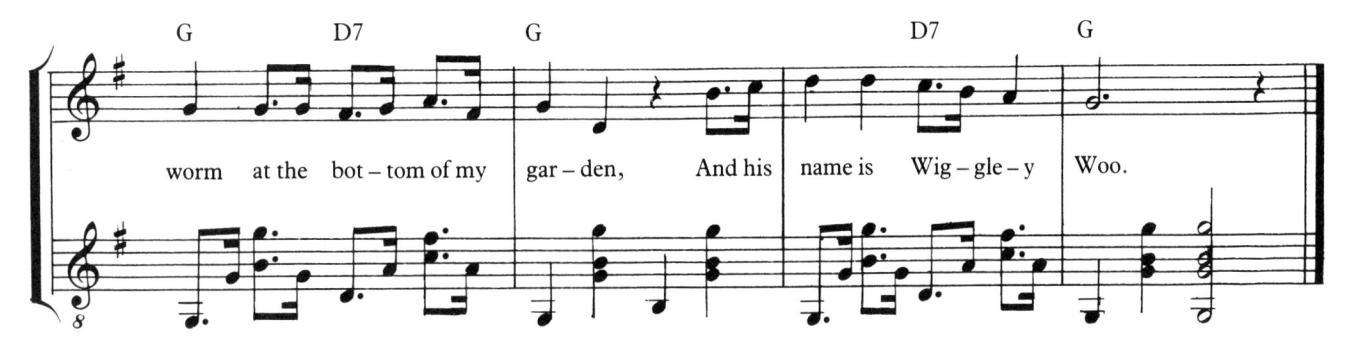

2. There's a worm at the bottom of my garden
And his name is Wiggley Woo.
There's a worm at the bottom of my garden
And all that he can do,
Is wiggle along and wiggle around

And wiggle himself back under the ground.
There's a worm at the bottom of my garden
And his name is Wiggley Woo.

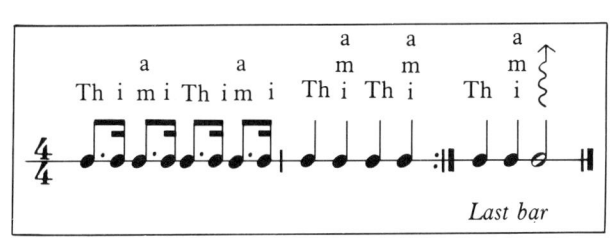

The descant recorder could play the melody.

Drum signals

Pass a small drum round the circle, while the teacher (leader) plays a pattern on another drum. Later the teacher (leader) could play on a tuned instrument. When the 'pattern' stops the person holding the drum either marks the pulse or, if they can, copies the pattern until the teacher picks it up again. Then the drum continues round the circle. Ensure everyone has a turn. The teacher should change the pattern at times to keep everyone alert.

Under a stone where the earth was firm
 (*Use forefinger for worm, cover with clenched fist of other hand for stone.*)
I found a little wriggly worm.
 (*Lift stone and worm wriggles away.*)
'Hello,' I said, 'How are you today?'
 (*Worm wriggles all over the place, or people.*)
But the wriggly worm just wriggled away.

There was a young lady called Maggie
Whose dog was enormous and shaggy:
 The front end of him
 looked ferocious and grim –
But the tail end was friendly and waggy.

Mr Tortoise

Someone is stirring in his nest of hay,
Someone pushes soft soil and dead leaves away;
Up into the sunshine comes a little nose,
Off into the garden Mr Tortoise goes.

His hard shell is heavy, he can only creep,
All through the winter he has lain asleep,
Waiting for the sunshine to send the snow away
And let him take a walk on a fine spring day.

R. Pope

Movement suggestions

Lines 1 and 2. Children gradually stir and make gentle, firm, pushing movements with heads and trunks.
Lines 3 and 4. Children begin slow, heavy movements which continue in the second verse.

(Poem and movement suggestion from *Poems for Movement*, published by Evans)

There are many learning situations to be derived from either a real tortoise or pictures of one. If there is not one in school or in one of the children's homes, see if you could borrow one for a day. Where does the tortoise come from (*not* counting the pet shop)? Does it sleep all winter? What is this called? Why the soil, leaves and hay? Continue to the ability level of the children.

Apple song

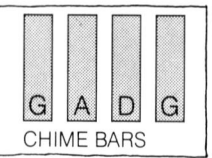

Gwen Rosman

Steadily
INTRODUCTION

CHIME BARS

Slower.... a tempo

1. I bought a bag of ap-ples, and dropped them, what a loss! A car ran them o-ver, Squish! Squash! Ap-ple sauce!

2 I bought a bag of oranges
     and dropped them, what a loss!
   A car ran them over
     squish, squash, orange squash.

3 I bought a bag of cherries,
     and dropped them with a slam!
   A car ran them over
     bim, bam, cherry jam.

4 I bought a bag of potatoes,
     and dropped them with a crash,
   A bus ran them over

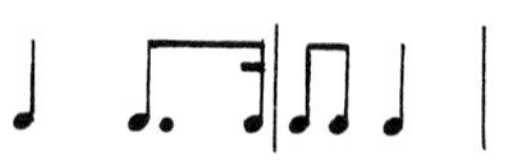

   biff, bash, potato mash.

Sing the 'squish, squash' etc. with obvious vocal relish!

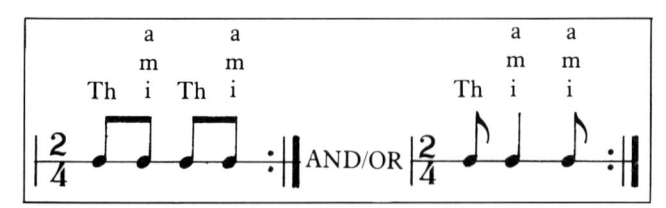

Stirring the Christmas pudding

Put the bowl upon the table,
Stir as smoothly as you're able.
Stir and wish, and stir and wish,
This is what you have to do,
To make your Christmas wish come true.

Stir the sugar, flour and fruit,
Silver charms so small and cute.
Stir and wish, and stir and wish.
Softly to myself I say,
'I hope it snows on Christmas Day.'

Grace Hamblin

Oh, I wish I'd looked after my teeth

Oh, I wish I'd looked after my teeth,
And spotted the perils beneath,
All the toffees I chewed,
And the sweet sticky food,
Oh, I wish I'd looked after my teeth.

Oh, I showed them the toothpaste all right,
I flashed it about late at night,
But up-and-down brushin'
And pokin' and fussin'
Didn't seem worth the time – I could bite!

If I'd known I was paving the way
To cavities, caps and decay,
The murder of fillin's
Injections and drillin's,
I'd have thrown all me sherbet away.

How I laughed at my mother's false teeth,
As they foamed in the waters beneath.
But now comes the reckonin'
It's me they are beckonin'
Oh, I wish I'd looked after my teeth.

Pam Ayres (Extract)

Table manners

The Goops they lick their fingers,
And the Goops they lick their knives;
They spill their broth on the table-cloth;
Oh, they live untidy lives.
The Goops they talk while eating,
And loud and fast they chew,
So that is why I am glad that I
Am not a Goop. Are you?

Gelett Burgess

Chips

Out of the paper bag
Comes the hot breath of the chips
And I shall blow on them
To stop them burning my lips.

Before I leave the counter
The woman shakes
Raindrops of vinegar on them
And salty snowflakes.

Outside the frosty pavements
Are slippery as a slide
But the chips and I
Are warm inside.

Stanley Cook

The ink is black

Tune: Earl Robinson
Words: David Arkin

Moderate
INTRODUCTION

1. The ink is black, the page is white, Together we learn to read and write, read and write. And now a child can understand, This is the law of all the land, all the land. The ink is black, the page is white, Together we learn to read and write, read and write.

2 The board is black, the chalk is white,
   The words stand out so clear and bright,
     clear and bright,
   And now at last we plainly see
   The alphabet of liberty,
   Liberty!
   The board is black, the chalk is white,
   The words stand out so clear and bright,
     clear and bright.

3 A child is black, a child is white,
   The whole world looks upon the sight,
   A beautiful sight.
   For very well the whole world knows,
   This is the way that freedom grows,
   Freedom grows!
   A child is black, a child is white,
   The whole world looks upon the sight,
   A beautiful sight.

4 The world is black, the world is white,
   It turns by day and then by night,
     then by night.
   It turns so each and everyone
   Can take his station in the sun,
   In the sun!
   The world is black, the world is white,
   Together we learn to read and write,
     read and write.

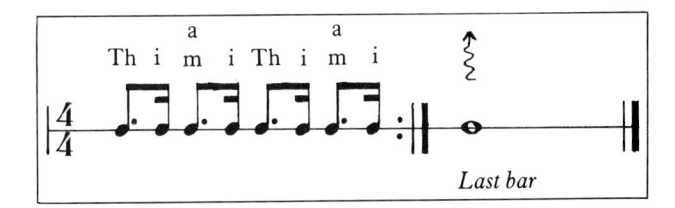

Circles

The white man drew a small circle in the sand
and told the red man,
'This is what the Indian knows,'
and drawing a big circle around the small one,
'This is what the white man knows.'

The Indian took the stick
and swept an immense ring around both circles:
'This is where the white man and the red man
know nothing.'

Carl Sandburg

Paper boats

Day by day I float my paper boats one by one down the running stream.
In big black letters I write my name on them and the name of the village where I live.
I hope that someone in some strange land will find them and know who I am.
I load my little boats with 'shiuli' flowers from our garden, and hope that these blooms of the dawn will be carried safely to land in the night.

Rabindranath Tagore

The past

Let no one say the past is dead,
The past is all about us and within,
Haunted by tribal memories, I know
This little now, this accidental present
Is not the all of me, whose long making
Is so much of the past.
Tonight here in suburbia I sit.
In easy chair before electric heater
Warmed by the red glow, I fall into dream:
I am away.
At the campfire in the bush, among
My own people, sitting on the ground.
No walls about me,
The stars over me.
The tall surrounding trees that stir in the wind
Making their own music,
Soft cries of the night coming to us, there
Where we are one with all old Nature's lives
Known and unknown,
In scenes where we belong but have now foresaken.
Deep chair and electric radiator
Are but since yesterday,
But a thousand camp-fires in the forest
Are in my blood.
Let none tell me the past is wholly gone.
Now is so small a part of time, so small a part
Of all the past years that have moulded me.

Kathleen Walker

Puff the magic dragon

Petter Yarrow

Not too fast
INTRODUCTION

VERSE / CHORUS

1. Puff the magic dragon lived by the sea, And frolicked in the autumn mist in a land called Honalee.

Puff the magic dragon lived by the sea, And frolicked in the autumn mist in a land called Honalee.

Little Jackie Paper loved that rascal Puff, And brought him strings and sealing wax and other fancy stuff.

Puff the magic dragon lived by the sea, And frolicked in the autumn mist in a land called Honalee.

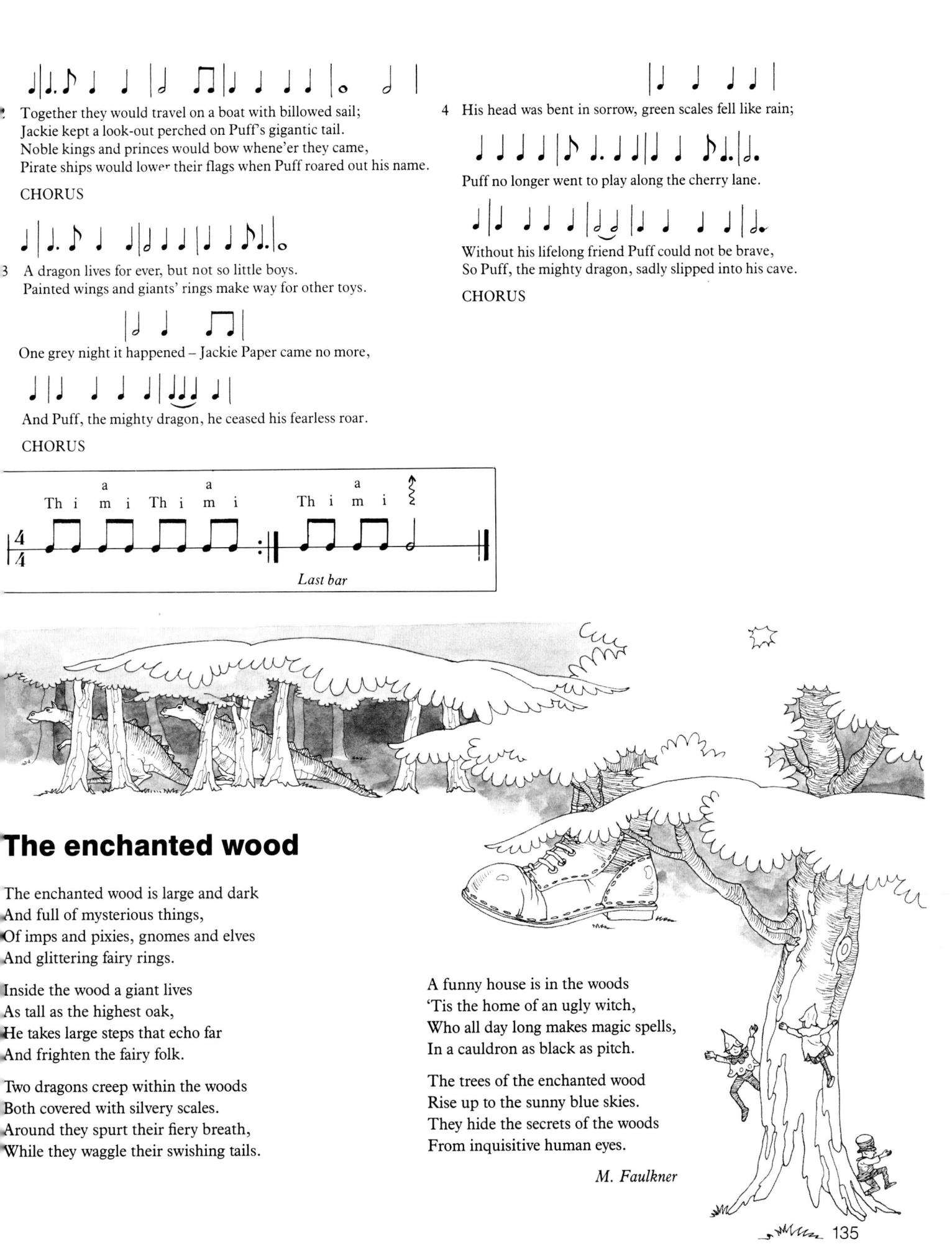

Together they would travel on a boat with billowed sail;
Jackie kept a look-out perched on Puff's gigantic tail.
Noble kings and princes would bow whene'er they came,
Pirate ships would lower their flags when Puff roared out his name.
CHORUS

3. A dragon lives for ever, but not so little boys.
   Painted wings and giants' rings make way for other toys.

One grey night it happened – Jackie Paper came no more,

And Puff, the mighty dragon, he ceased his fearless roar.
CHORUS

4. His head was bent in sorrow, green scales fell like rain;

Puff no longer went to play along the cherry lane.

Without his lifelong friend Puff could not be brave,
So Puff, the mighty dragon, sadly slipped into his cave.
CHORUS

The enchanted wood

The enchanted wood is large and dark
And full of mysterious things,
Of imps and pixies, gnomes and elves
And glittering fairy rings.

Inside the wood a giant lives
As tall as the highest oak,
He takes large steps that echo far
And frighten the fairy folk.

Two dragons creep within the woods
Both covered with silvery scales.
Around they spurt their fiery breath,
While they waggle their swishing tails.

A funny house is in the woods
'Tis the home of an ugly witch,
Who all day long makes magic spells,
In a cauldron as black as pitch.

The trees of the enchanted wood
Rise up to the sunny blue skies.
They hide the secrets of the woods
From inquisitive human eyes.

M. Faulkner

The magic seeds

There was an old woman who sowed a corn seed,
And from it there sprouted a tall yellow weed.
She planted the seeds of the tall yellow flower,
And up sprang a blue one in less than an hour,
The seeds of the blue one she sowed in a bed,
And up sprang a tall tree with blossoms of red.
And high in the treetop there sang a white bird,
And his song was the sweetest that ever was heard.
The people they came from far and from near,
The song of that little white bird for to hear.

James Reeves

Make a wall frieze, or collage, to illustrate the various events in the poem. The more fantastic and colourful the frieze is the better.

Flute Girl

Flute Girl, Flute Girl,
Sits by the sea.
Plays a sweet tune,
Plays a soft melody.

Flute Girl, Flute Girl,
Sits on the sand,
Sits, and her silver flute
Shines in her hand.

Flute Girl, Flute Girl,
Waits for the tide,
When her soft silver tune
Brings seals to her side.

Flute Girl, Flute Girl,
See the seals play,
Close by the shore
At the end of the day.

Seal Girl, Seal Girl,
Plays her sweet tune,
As the seals' silver ripples
Shine in the moon.

Roderick Hunt

Fafnir and the knights

In the quiet waters
Of the forest pool
Fafnir the dragon
His tongue will cool

His tongue will cool
And his muzzle dip
Until the soft waters lave
His muzzle tip

Happy simple creature
In his coat of mail
With a mild bright eye
And a waving tail

Happy the dragon
In the days expended
Before the time had come for dragons
To be hounded

The time has not come yet
But must come soon
Meanwhile happy Fafnir
Take thy rest in the afternoon

Take thy rest
Fafnir while thou mayest
In the long grass
Where thou liest

An extract from Stevie Smith's poem. The full poem has a very different feeling only hinted at in this extract.

The artist David Shepherd has done some marvellous paintings of elephants that occasionally appear in magazines, etc. If you can acquire some of them they make superb illustrative material for use with the children. He has also painted other animals and a series of railway engines. All excellent.

The elephant

The elephant carries a great big trunk;
He never packs it with clothes;
It has no lock and it has no key,
But he takes it wherever he goes.

Oliphaunt

Grey as a mouse,
Big as a house,
Nose like a snake,
I make the earth shake,
As I tramp through the grass;
Trees crack as I pass.
With horns in my mouth
I walk in the South,
Flapping big ears.
Beyond count of years
I stump round and round,
Never lie on the ground,
Not even to die.
Oliphaunt am I,
Biggest of all,
Huge, old, and tall.
If ever you'd met me,
You wouldn't forget me.
If you never do,
You won't think I'm true;
But old Oliphaunt am I,
And I never lie.

J. R. Tolkien

The elephant

The elephant walks like this, like that
He's terribly big and he's terribly fat.
He has no fingers, he has no toes,
But goodness gracious, WHAT A NOSE!

Read the poem to the children and ask them to mime how they think an elephant moves. If he's big and fat will he move very fast? Does he have *no* toes? What is the name for his nose? What does he use it for? Is there anything else you know about elephants?

Actions

1 Lift feet high, bending knees, and place on ground very slowly and carefully. (Children with little mobility use hands or knees on a table or similar, lifting them as high as possible, then slowly and carefully putting them down again.)
2 Stretch up as high as possible.
3 Stretch out as wide as possible.
4 Move fingers, holding up hands.
5 Bend down and touch toes.
6 Make a big (reversed 'S') shape with your hand from your nose to as near the ground as you can. Take lots of room and move as much of you as possible. Some adaptation is needed (see above) for children with less mobility than others.

Nellie the elephant

Ralph Butler and Peter Hart

To Bombay a travelling circus came. They brought an intelligent elephant, Nellie was her name. One dark night she slipped her iron chain, and off she ran to Hindustan and was never seen again. Nellie the elephant packed her trunk and said good-bye to the circus. Off she went with a trumpety trump. Trump! trump!

A A7 D G D
trump! Nel – lie the e – le – phant packed her trunk and trun – dled back to the jun – gle.
rall. a tempo
Em D G A7 D D7 G
Off she went with a trum – pe – ty trump. Trump! trump! trump! The head of the herd was
D G D E A
call – ing far, far a – way. They met one night in the sil – ver light on the
molto rall. a tempo
E7 A A7 D G
road to Man – de – lay. So Nel-lie the e – le – phant packed her trunk and said good – bye to the
D Em D G A7 D
cir – cus. Off she went with a trum – pe – ty trump. Trump! trump! trump!
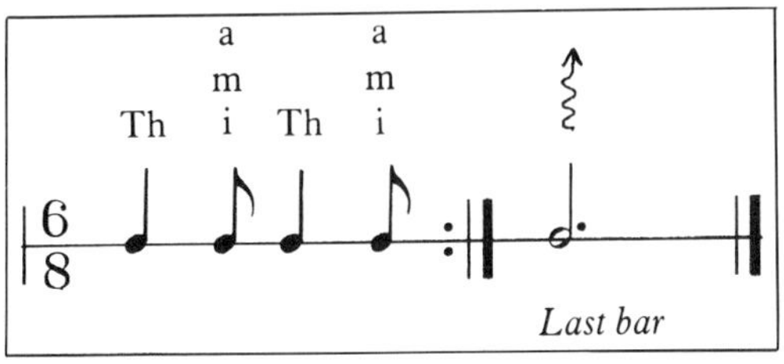
a a
m m
Th i Th i
Last bar

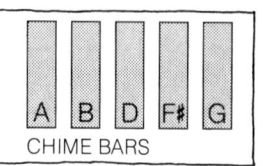

Popeye the sailorman

Sammy Lerner

Moderate, waltz time

1. I'm Popeye the sailorman, I live in a caravan. I opened the door and fell flat on the

floor, ___ I'm Pop-eye the sai — lor man. ___

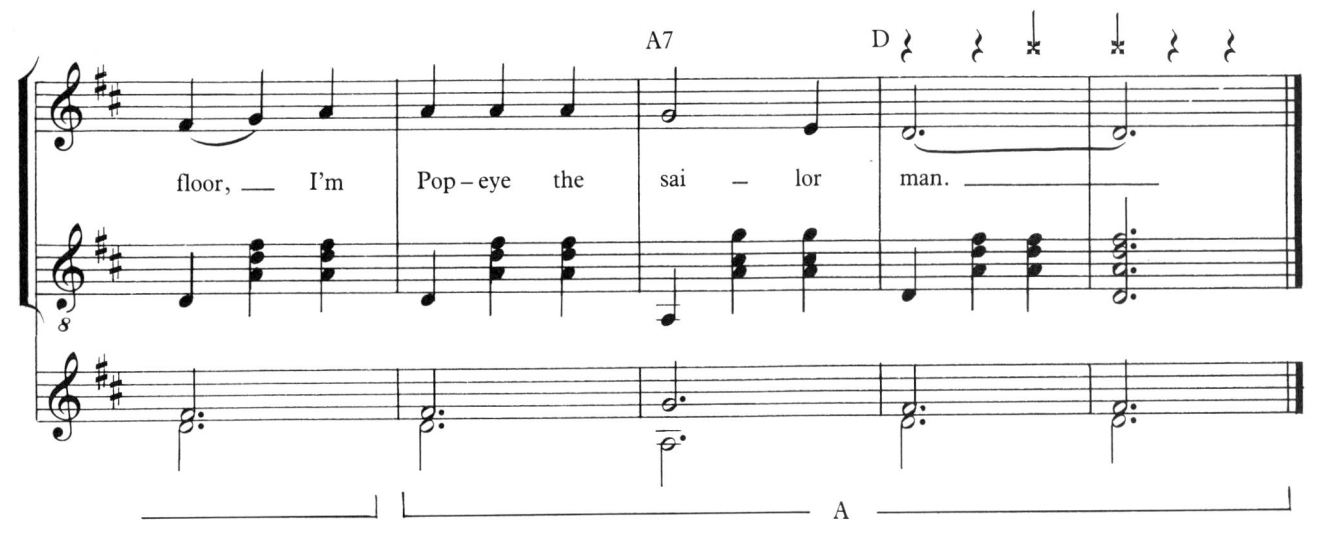

I'm Popeye the sailor man,
I'm Popeye the sailor man,
I'm strong to the finish
   'cause I eats my spinach
I'm Popeye the sailor man.

I'm Popeye the sailor man,
I'm Popeye the sailor man,
I love to go swimmin'
   with bare naked wimmin
I'm Popeye the sailor man.

Add other verses as desired.

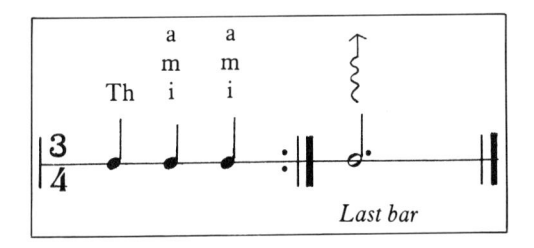

The descant recorder could play the melody. Clap on the asterisks (or make some other sound in each verse).

The chime bar part is in two patterns, **A** and **B**.
A = D – A7 – D – D. **B** = G – G – D – D

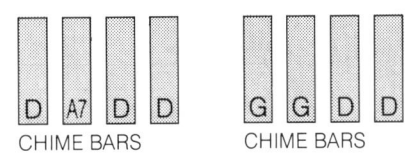

If possible lay out in two sets, and have two children play. Once child plays pattern **A** and the other pattern **B**. The Introduction is pattern **A**, then for each verse play patterns **A** – **B** – **B** – **A**. Pattern **A** is IN – OUT – IN – IN. Pattern **B** is OUT – OUT – IN – IN.

The growing river

At first the river's very small,
And can't float anything at all;
But later, as it journeys on,
It's large enough to float a swan.

It grows till it can safely float
A slim canoe and then a boat;
And later still, as like as not,
It manages to float a yacht.

And presently, when really large,
It takes a steamer, then a barge,
And last it passes busy quays
And floats great ships to foreign seas.

Rodney Bennett

The tide in the river

The tide in the river,
The tide in the river,
The tide in the river runs deep,
I saw a shiver
Pass over the river
As the tide turned in its sleep.

Eleanor Farjeon

Up, up and away

Without hurrying

INTRODUCTION

Jim Webb

Would you like __ to ride in my beau-ti-ful bal-loon? __ Would you like __ to glide in my beau-ti-ful balloon? __ We could sing a song and sail a-long in the sil-ver sky, for we can fly. __

Up, up, up — and a-way in my beau-ti-ful bal-loon.

2 I would like to ride in your beautiful balloon,
   I would like to glide in your beautiful balloon,
   We could sing a song and sail along
     in the silver sky, for we can fly,
   Up, up, up and away in this beautiful balloon.

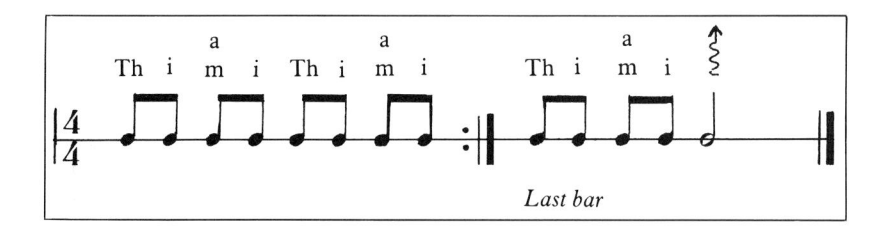

Clouds

Wonder where they come from?
Wonder where they go?
Wonder why they're sometimes high
and sometimes hanging low?
Wonder what they're made of,
and if they weigh a lot?
Wonder if the sky feels bare
up there
when clouds are not?

Aileen Fisher

The spinning earth

The earth, they say,
spins round and round.
It doesn't look it
from the ground and never makes
a spinning sound.

And water never swirls
and swishes
from oceans full
of dizzy fishes,
and shelves don't lose
their pans and dishes.

And houses don't go whirling by,
or puppies swirl around the sky,
or robins spin instead of fly.

It may be true
what people say
about one spinning
night and day . . . . . .
but I keep wondering, anyway.

Aileen Fisher

It's dark outside

It's dark outside.
It's dark inside.
It's dark behind the door.

I wonder
if I'm brave enough
to walk across the floor.

I am –
at least I think I am.
I'll try it once and see

if Mum comes up
or stays downstairs
with Dad and cups of tea.

Nancy Chambers

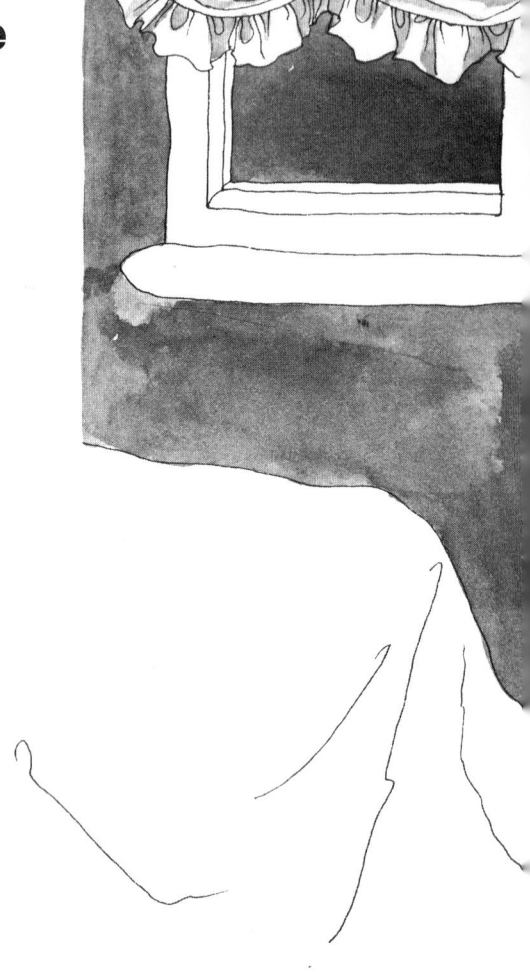

Lonely boy

Lonely boy, lonely boy
Let me play with you
I'm on my own
I'm all alone
And you've nobody too.

John Kitching

I saw a man pursuing the horizon

I saw a man pursuing the horizon;
Round and round they sped.
I was disturbed at this;
I accosted the man.
'It is futile,' I said,
'You can never –'
'You lie,' he cried,
And ran on.

Stephen Crane

The most I can do for my friend is simply to be his friend.

Thoreau (1817–1862)

Printed and bound in Great Britain by William Clowes Limited, Beccles and London